Making Brilliant Presentations

Structuring and Delivering Superb Presentations Every Time

About the Author

Lynda Byron is a senior management specialist at the Irish Management Institute. She specialises in the areas of personal development and customer service. She has been designing and delivering much sought-after courses on presentations skills for many years. Lynda also works with individuals and has coached many people at the top level of organisations to reach their full potential as presenters and communicators.

Lynda's unique style of teaching helps executives at all levels to build confidence and excellence in their skills of presenting by creating a safe and enjoyable learning environment. She helps individuals to realise their own strengths and areas for improvement by giving focused but sensitive feedback. She is an NLP Master Practitioner, a keen advocate of theatre-based training, an avid storyteller and uses a wide range of these techniques to help business people excel at what they do.

Lynda recently featured on the Ray D'Arcy Show, on Today FM, helping one of his listeners to get over their phobia of public speaking.

About Owen and Brian

Brian Colbert and Owen Fitzpatrick are experienced master practitioners and trainers in NLP. They run refreshingly practical NLP workshops that really help people learn about NLP and use it in their everyday life and in coaching and training others.

Many of the techniques in this book have a basis in NLP. Owen and Brian have helped me to make sense of them and to put them into a palatable form between these pages.

I am indebted to both of them for their helpful feedback on the first edition and the ideas they gave me, as well as the ongoing support for this, the second edition. It probably would never have seen the light of day if it weren't for their perseverance.

If you want to look further in this area, I would urge you to take a look at their website: www.nlp.ie. Give yourself a treat and attend one of their courses. They really can change your life!

Making Brilliant Presentations

Structuring and Delivering Superb Presentations Every Time

LYNDA BYRON

This book was typeset by Gilbert Gough Typesetting for
Blackhall Publishing
33 Carysfort Avenue
Blackrock
Co. Dublin
Ireland
e-mail: info@blackhallpublishing.com
www.blackhallpublishing.com

ISBN: 1 842180 55 X

A catalogue record for this book is available from the British Library.

Printed in Ireland by
ColourBooks Ltd

To Sandra and Sinead – the best daughters ever

and

Frank – the wind beneath my wings

Contents

Acknowledgements

Thanks to my family and friends who were a constant source of support and encouragement.

To my employer, the Irish Management Institute, and particularly the rest of the members of the Faculty for their help and encouragement.

To Brian and Owen who taught me so much and made me write the new edition.

To Gerry O'Connor of Blackhall Publishing for his patience.

Introduction

This book is for everyone who has to make presentations. It assumes nothing except that you want to improve your skills and make an impact on your audiences.

We all feel differently when faced with the opportunity to present. But this book starts with a very common feeling – fear. This can come in many forms but the best presenters will feel some nerves. This comes from the respect they have for their audiences and actually helps them to make brilliant presentations.

The rest of the book brings you through a structured approach to preparing and delivering presentations with impact, giving you hints and tips as well as tried and tested techniques.

I hope you find it useful.

CHAPTER ONE

Handling the Fear

This chapter will you help you to:

- Realise that nerves are a normal part of presenting
- See the positive side of nerves
- Control and hide the nerves from your audience.

The presentation is tomorrow. Ten o'clock sharp. You are talking to the management group, or worse still, the board. They are unfriendly. You do not know them very well. But you must persuade them. You have to get them to decide on this issue. They must support your idea.

But have you done enough to prepare? Do you know what you are talking about? Do any of them know more than you do on this issue? Every time you think about it your stomach lurches, your palms sweat – panic is beginning to set in.

Going to bed, you wonder why you bother – you are not going to sleep anyway. You will toss and turn for hours, picturing their bored or hostile faces as you lie there. Finally you nod off. The shrill alarm wakes you at 8.00 a.m. But you have only just got to sleep. You suddenly remember what is happening at ten o'clock. OH NO! How will you cope? Breakfast? You must be joking!

You drive to the office, grab a coffee and head for the meeting. Standing outside, the shakes start, your scalp is sweating, your stomach is doing somersaults, you feel sick. Your mouth is dry. Why is your tongue sticking to the roof of your mouth? You just know when you start to speak your voice will come out in a quiver. You just want to go home – forget the whole idea. Two weeks ago it seemed like a great opportunity. Wow, presenting to the board – me! Now all you can see is the wonderful chance of making an absolute fool of yourself.

"Please, please let them cancel the meeting, let me off the hook," you pray. The door opens – "You're on." Oh God!

Does any of this feel even vaguely familiar? If you have ever presented, I bet it does.

Everyone who makes presentations – no matter how often they do it, how good they are, what level they are in the company – feels nervous before making a presentation. That is if they are any good: it's normal, it's okay, it's necessary. If you are not nervous you cannot possibly perform well as a presenter.

There is a positive and a negative side of nerves. Nerves get the adrenalin going. When the adrenalin starts pumping around your body, different things happen. We are all familiar with the negative side: butterflies in the stomach, sweating, shaking, twitching, stuttering, dry mouth, wobbly voice, red rash that rises from the neck up through the face and all the rest. I guarantee you have felt a large proportion of them yourself. You can control these and you must.

> ***Word to the Wise***
>
> Nerves are an essential part of presenting well. The adrenalin rush that being nervous brings gives you that essential energy and passion which you need.

Understanding these side-effects can be helpful. Try thinking about why this is happening to your body. Your ancestors were hunters who had to feed their families, and the same instincts are still alive in you. Imagine while you are hunting you come face to face with a large bear. You are frightened. Your body helps you out by releasing adrenalin, the fight or flight chemical. This pumps blood from your extremities to your vital organs, making your heart beat faster and your hands sweaty and shaky. It closes down anything that is not necessary, like your saliva glands, for instance, so your mouth dries up, and it narrows your focus so all you can see is the bear. The adrenalin makes you concentrate on what is really important for your survival at that moment and gives you the strength to handle it.

The same happens when you get nervous before a presentation. Your body senses your fear and tries to help you out. The positive side is less obvious to the presenter but very obvious to the audience. As the adrenalin pumps you get energy. This energy encourages your enthusiasm and passion. A presenter who is nervous but is controlling their nerves well, is interesting, exciting and easy to listen to; a presenter who is lethargic, lacks energy and enthusiasm, and does not seem to care about the subject is boring to listen to and appears to be just "going through the motions". Which type of presenter would you rather be?

So, go with it. The adrenalin will give you an edge. It will allow you to focus sharply on your topic and give you a buzz that will help you connect strongly with your audience. Do not be afraid of the side-effects. Instead, use them to help you to be a brilliant, focused and energetic presenter.

Facing the Fear

Ask yourself what you are really afraid of. What is the worst thing that can happen?

Common answers are:

- Making a fool of myself
- The equipment breaking down
- Not being able to answer questions
- Hostile audiences
- Being in the limelight – all the focus is on me
- Making a bad impression
- Panicking when I look at the audience
- Jokes going flat
- Boring the audience
- If I make a bad presentation, my boss will think I cannot do my job either.

All of these fears can be handled by preparing your presentation meticulously, checking your equipment carefully and delivering with skill. The rest of this book looks at how you can avoid the above pitfalls and learn these skills. Presenting is a learned skill. Anybody can make a good presentation once they are prepared to put the work into it. But first you need to manage yourself so that you avoid the worst symptoms of nerves being shown to your audience.

Controlling your Nerves

Being nervous is good – in fact it is essential for any good presenter – but you must control your nerves. Usually, the worst effects of nerves subside after the first few minutes of a presentation if you are well prepared because you will have already started to get a positive response from the audience and know you are going to do well. There are numerous ways you can help yourself.

Imagine yourself Succeeding

All too often when we are asked to make a presentation, we imagine all the pitfalls, the things that can and will inevitably go wrong. Why not picture yourself in front of that group of people looking confident, smiling and in control. Is that so hard? When I started presenting first, I used to be afraid of the audience reaction. I was so afraid that they would feel sorry for me. I couldn't bear to think of their sympathetic faces, saying to themselves, "Ah God love her, she's very nervous". That was my worst nightmare. You may have a different bad dream in your mind. However, I now picture all the groups I talk to as having happy, smiling faces. They are all enjoying the presentation; they are all interested. That is what keeps me going. If you appear confident and seem to be enjoying the presentation, it is highly likely that your audience will enjoy listening to you. Think of things you do well, the things you are really good at; try to capture the feelings you get when you are succeeding at that activity and transpose them onto your presentation. Try it; it's not as far-fetched as you think. See Chapter 4 for an exercise you can try.

> ***Word to the Wise***
>
> If you appear confident and seem to be enjoying the presentation, it is highly likely that your audience will enjoy listening to you.

Think of your Audience as Friendly, not Hostile

Think about how you feel when you are a member of an audience. Are you hoping that the presenter will die on their feet or do you hope they will be interesting? Usually, an audience is hoping for a good presentation. They are not automatically hostile. In fact, sometimes the audience is almost as nervous as you. They may be asked a question that they cannot answer or to make a decision and are hoping you will give them enough information for them to make it well. Give them the benefit of the doubt. Remember, your behaviour can influence theirs: if you behave as though you are confident and enjoying yourself, they will expect you to make an excellent presentation. If you look nervous and worried they may expect you to get it wrong.

Certainly, there may be one or two people in your audience who may be hostile towards you. Try to work out who they could be in advance and why. It is possible that they do not feel that you should have been asked to present at all; maybe they feel they should have been asked. You need to flatter these people in front of the rest of the audience and make them feel good about you being up there. You need to turn them around. (In Chapter 9, you will find some tips on handling some of these hostile behaviours.)

Relax, Chill Out

Deep breathing can help you while you are waiting for your turn to present. Ensure you are breathing from your whole chest, taking in deep breaths and letting them out slowly. Take a few minutes on your own just before you start. Leave the room, find a quiet corner and contemplate your navel for five minutes. Go over your opening lines and try to remember what you are going to say next. This will give you more confidence. Now you are ready to face the group. (See Chapter 4 for more on this.)

Beating the Shakes

When the adrenalin starts pumping in advance of a presentation, it can cause a trembling in your body. This can be at its worst in your hands. Everyone can see you tremble; everything you pick up seems to wobble; you try to drink a glass of water to calm you down and you spill it all down your front; you drop your notes and slides all over the floor; the red dot of your laser pointer runs all over the screen. This is one of the most visible aspects of the negative side of nerves and is something you must control.

If your hands are shaking, avoid holding pieces of paper, slides or cards in your hands, as these make your hands appear larger and the shake more exaggerated. Leave paper down on a side table and only pick up slides when you need to use them. Do everything with very definite and obvious movements: this will make you appear more confident. When you are changing slides on the overhead projector hold them firmly with two hands: this will stop them wobbling.

We often need to point at particular figures on a slide; if your hands are shaking, do not use your finger to point as it will show up on the screen as gigantic and out of control. Instead, try placing a pen down on the slide, using that same definite movement to point to the relevant spot. Make sure the pen has a clip or square edges so that it does not roll off the overhead projector and make it even more awkward for you. If you are using infra-red remote control with an LCD presentation, be careful not to leave your finger on the button that changes slides. If you are shaky, you are likely to change the slides by mistake, rushing past two or three slides at a time. The audience will notice this. So keep your finger off the button when you are not actually using it.

What about those legs? Did you ever get a wobble in one knee that you cannot seem to stop? There it is – knee shaking like crazy and your foot leaping about all over the place. Try shaking out your knees before you go into the room to help relax them and keep walking around. Remember, it is only when you stand still that your knees will shake.

Wipe Out the Trembling Voice

You have your opening line all worked out, well prepared, meticulously rehearsed and then you look at the audience and all that comes out is a little wobbly voice – "Good morning everyone" – that no one can hear and that destroys any last shred of confidence you may have had left. How can you possibly go on after that? This has not really made the impact you had intended. Luckily, there is a very simple solution to this common problem. If you say your first line loudly, boom it out, you will find that not only will it grab the attention of your audience, it will also be a physical impossibility for your voice to tremble – there will be too much force behind it! It will have the added advantage of making you feel in control and in command of your audience. There are also numerous voice exercises you can try which will help you to feel more confident about your voice (see Chapter 8).

Dry Mouth

If you suffer from dry mouth you will experience an uncomfortable time while you are talking: your tongue sticks to the roof of your mouth, your lips feel like sandpaper and are welded together, and your gums are itchy. Sounds lovely. When we feel this coming on we usually reach for a glass of water to try to lubricate the mouth as quickly as possible. This can be dangerous when standing in front of a group. It is a bit like trying to drink a glass of water having just been to the dentist for a filling: you are likely to miss your mouth altogether and pour the liquid all down your front. That's all you need!

An altogether safer remedy is to conjure up a picture in your mind. While you are reading this, imagine you are going to the fridge and taking out a big, juicy lemon. Put this down on a chopping board on a nearby worktop and cut it down the middle with a sharp knife. The juice is flooding out of the lemon onto the board. Now, pick up one half of the lemon and squeeze the juice into a glass. Are you salivating? If this is working for you now, it will also work during a presentation. Once you have done this once, all you need is the picture of the lemon in your mind to bring back the memory of the juice and you will be drooling in no time. No more dry mouth problems.

Creeping, Red Rash

Many women, in particular, complain of a creeping, red rash: red blotches that start on their chest and creep up their neck and finally onto their face. If you are a sufferer, always make sure you are wearing a high neck blouse or a shirt with a scarf in the neck. This will cover the rash for a while. Hopefully just knowing that your audience cannot see your embarrassment will be enough to make the rash subside before it reaches the facial area. If, however, it has a habit of continuing its journey above the jawline, then invest in some make-up with a slight green tinge. Your local beautician or pharmacy will advise you on the best one for you.

Do's and Don'ts

Don't worry about being nervous – it's a good thing
Don't assume the audience is out to get you
Don't think you will be a star without putting in the work

Do face your fears – we all have them
Do capitalise on your nerves by using them to make an energetic presentation
Do learn to manage your nerves

Chapter Two

Building Credibility

This chapter will help you to:

- Understand why credibility is important in a speaker
- See how you can become an expert
- Learn to be yourself
- Work on your image.

Imagine yourself in DIY mode at home. You have been intending to put a set of shelves on the wall in the kitchen for months now and finally you have decided that today is the day. The shelves are lying on the floor, the drill is out of the box on the kitchen table but you don't know which type of screws to use. So it's off to the local DIY store for advice. At the counter, you explain your problem to Charlie. You have three shelves, three foot long and five inches wide. You have bought wrought-iron brackets but you need advice on which screws you need to fix them to the wall. The scruffy assistant looks at you vaguely, shakes his head, scratches his chin and mumbles distractedly, "Weeeeelllll, you could try these ones, or maybe these would be better … I suppose these would do you." He hands you a packet of pre-packed steel screws. Do you think you have got good advice? Would you do what he suggests or would you seek a second opinion? I would be inclined to ask someone else; after all, he didn't look or sound very confident, did he?

As a contrast, think about an assistant in another hardware store, Jimmy. He is smartly dressed, casual but clean and tidy. He smiles when you approach him. When you explain the same problem, Jimmy asks a few questions to get the necessary information first: "What type of wall are you attaching them to?" "What will you be putting on the shelves?" "What tools do you have to do the job?" When he has collected all the information, he says in a confident voice, "If I were doing that job, I'd use these screws with the rawlplugs. You can't go wrong." Would you feel more confident with this approach? I bet you would.

What makes Jimmy credible and Charlie not credible? Jimmy is an expert. He has personal experience of putting up shelves – he told you as much. He looks confident, he sounds confident, he *is* confident. He

has done his homework. He knows his stuff. Charlie has probably never put up shelves in his life. He does not know what he is doing. He looks and sounds as though he is making it up, as though he cannot be trusted.

There is a similarity between the above example and a presenter. I am sure you have watched a presentation where the speaker is vague, does not seem to know what they are talking about and stumbles through even the simplest of explanations. The impression they give is unprofessional and not credible. Usually, this puts us off and stops us from taking them seriously.

How do you come across? Do you always do your homework? Are you an expert in your subject? You need to be. Would you prefer to be a Charlie or a Jimmy?

If we are listening to a Charlie-type presenter, we don't always believe what they are saying to us. We feel irritated by them. We sometimes get hostile because we feel that Charlie does not have enough respect for us to bother coming prepared. We don't respect him because he does not appear to respect us. We are more likely to ask difficult questions to expose this unprofessional speaker. Remember, people buy people. If we want our audience to listen to what we are saying, we need to show them we really care about them.

If you want to build credibility with your audience, you must both become an expert and appear to be an expert.

Word to the Wise

Be an expert, look like an expert … People like to think they are listening to an expert.

Be an Expert

You need to start by doing your homework.

Find out all you can about your subject. Read around the topic, ask lots of people, try things out, experience as much as you can. All of this will give you confidence and make you more of an expert.

You may be asked to speak about a subject you feel you are an expert in. This is good – look for these opportunities and take all of them. But you must prepare very well, even if you know all there is to know. (See Chapter 3.)

Sometimes, however, you may be asked to speak about a topic that is a little alien to your background or line of work. If it is something you can find out about and you have time to do your homework, that is okay. Work hard at becoming very knowledgeable on the subject and you will be fine. If you are asked to make one of these presentations tomorrow … refuse. When you do not have the time to research properly, you are doomed to fail. You are only setting yourself up to make a fool of yourself. Don't fall into this trap.

There are also subjects that you will never be able to get to grips with, no matter how much time you have and no matter how hard you try. This is another case where you should refuse. You were probably asked because someone has heard you speak on your pet subject and you were brilliant. This does not mean that you can be brilliant on any topic. It is flattering to be asked but if you cannot do it well, you should not even try.

The main message, therefore, is if you are happy that you can be an expert, you should take the opportunity to present. If you cannot be knowledgeable on the topic, leave it to someone else. Do not let yourself be talked into presenting on a subject that you do not feel comfortable with – it will only damage your credibility and your confidence. If you can match their needs with your strengths, you are in business. It's a question of fit.

In the last chapter, we spoke about having passion for your subject; this passion is an essential part of being a good presenter. If you are passionate about a subject, take as many opportunities that come your way to present on it. You will build your credibility as a speaker in this way.

But remember, nobody knows everything about a subject. Nobody is expecting you to know everything. If you are asked a question that you cannot answer, be honest and say so. It is quite legitimate to tell your enquirer that you had not thought about that aspect before and to ask them if they would mind if you checked it up and got back to them. Usually, this makes them feel good that they thought of a question that the "expert" had not even considered before. If you handle them sensitively they will admire your honesty and your real enthusiasm for your subject. By the way, if you say you will get back to them, be sure you do.

Be Yourself

Be yourself when presenting. You have all seen wonderful presenters in action who command the attention of the audience effortlessly. You would love to be like them: unruffled, confident and in control. They look and sound good. You wonder if you could ever be like them. A mistake that presenters often make is trying to mimic other good presenters. You must be yourself. You have huge strengths – use them to your advantage. If you try to be like someone else you will lose your strengths. You probably won't be able to mimic their good parts well enough so, ultimately, you will lose credibility with your audience because you look and sound like a fake.

> ***Word to the Wise***
>
> Never try to present like someone you admire. Be Yourself. The audience will see through you otherwise.

Everyone can be a good presenter. I do not believe it is a skill we are born with; it is a learned skill. Learn what your strengths are and find out what your little problems are so that you can correct them. You will be a good presenter when you really put the work into it. Certainly it comes a little more naturally to some than to others. There are only a select few who can be brilliant, charismatic presenters without much effort, but all of us can be professional, interesting and credible.

Look the Part

How do people perceive you? How would you like to be perceived by your audience?

Imagine yourself sitting in a pub, chatting to a friend. The door opens and in walks a man who is dressed a little strangely, maybe has long hair, very loud-coloured clothes and big boots. You see him walking past you while there is a lull in the conversation. Think about your reaction. Usually, what we do is pass a remark to our friend: "Who's your man? He's weird!" Now, think about what made you say that. You don't know this man or anything about him. You don't actually know he is weird. All you know about him is that he is dressed a little strangely. What you have just done is to make a judgement about a person by the way he is dressed.

Audiences do this en masse. Everything that the audience can see of you can help them make up their minds about whether you are credible. They will look at your clothes, your hair, your shoes and if they are close enough even your finger nails. Your grooming and dress need to be appropriate to the audience and to the image you want to portray. Usually, a good rule of thumb is that you should be at least as well dressed as the best-dressed person in the room. This shows respect for the audience. For example, if you are presenting to a group of business people, it would be appropriate to wear a suit. But here you have to be careful. If you never wear a suit because you are an artistic type of person working in that line of work, a business suit may be the wrong choice. In this case a smart version of your artistic clothes would be more appropriate.

Some invitations to speak bear the instructions "Dress Casual". Watch out: this is dangerous. Dress casual to you may mean jeans and a jumper but to someone else who may be in your audience it may just mean not wearing their best tie. If in doubt, always err on the side of dressing up rather than down. If you turn up to a presentation in a suit and discover that all of your audience is in casual clothes, it is very easy to take off the jacket and tie, loosen the collar of the shirt and roll up your sleeves. Now you are casual – just like them. It is, however, impossible to turn a jeans and jumper into a smart suit, no matter how hard you try.

It is important to see yourself as your audience will see you. Sometimes seeing yourself on video can help with this. You get used to seeing yourself in the mirror in that crumpled suit with your hair a little too long and specks of mud on your shoes. You do not notice these little things any more. Recording yourself on video even for a few minutes can be very revealing. It is something I notice when I work with groups of managers. When they see themselves on video the first thing they notice is the fact that they need a haircut or that their shirt was hanging out. It helps us to see ourselves as others do.

Do not fall into the trap of rushing out to buy a new outfit for a presentation and wear it for the first time standing in front of one hundred people. That is the wrong time to discover that there is an itchy label that is tearing the skin off your neck every time you move. It is also too late to discover that the hem has not been stitched properly and is hanging down for all to see. Try to wear the outfit in advance to make sure all is well and it really does look as smart as it is intended to. The same goes for shoes: it is hard to be persuasive when your feet are killing you and your new shoes are squeaking.

Clothes can be distracting. If you want the audience to remember you and what you are saying rather than your fashion sense, avoid wearing an outrageously coloured tie or a loud suit. Wear something that is professional, smart and won't take away from what you are saying. Patterns make you blink. Every time you blink, it takes away from your brain's concentration on the topic. Do not buy fabrics that will shine under bright lights. A subtle pattern like a light pin stripe is fine in a fabric with a matt finish.

Different colours say different things about you. A black suit may make you look extremely authoritative but it may also give the impression that you are arrogant and power-hungry. A better selection would be dark navy or dark grey with a crisp white or pale blue shirt and a smart tie.

However, your image will only help you at the start of your presentation. If you look awful and make a wonderful presentation, you will still be rated much more highly than if you look great and make a terrible presentation.

A Special Word for Women

It is a little more difficult for a woman to look authoritative but always possible through the right selection of clothes, shoes and make-up. Don't feel you have to "power dress". It is not essential or even desirable to dress like a man. Women should always wear a tailored suit when presenting if they want to appear professional. Knitted suits, cardigans and knitted waistcoats just do not have the same effect. Navy or dark grey suits with pretty, not over-fussy blouses or shirts look smart and neat. Watch out for anything that is frilly, as this can create the wrong impression. Don't overdo the jewellery either: a simple brooch, small earrings and a plain chain around the neck are sufficient; any more might be distracting.

Make-up should look natural and not overdone. Comfortable shoes are a must. A small heel can help to boost your confidence and help you to look smarter. However, don't wear great big heels to make you appear taller: you could find it difficult to move quickly enough. Remember, when we get nervous, we also get clumsy. You really don't want to fall off your shoes in front of a group of people. It tends to take the credibility away a little.

Do's and Don'ts

Don't present on a topic you are not comfortable with
Don't wear uncomfortable or distracting clothes

Do your homework - be an expert
Do decide what image you want to portray
Do show respect for your audience by how you look and by preparing well

Chapter Three

Preparing Well for a Presentation

This chapter will help you to:

- Set clear objectives
- Tailor your presentation to your audience
- Arrange your content for effect
- Rehearse for the big day.

Setting Realistic Objectives

Remember when you were at school or at college and exams were coming up? The teachers or lecturers would beat into you that you must first read and then answer the question; that you should not waffle all around the topic or just write all you know about the general subject area; and that you must show the examiner that not only do you know the subject but you understand it well enough to be able to answer a specific question on it. What did we do? Most of us, at any rate, decided to ignore the good advice of our teachers and put everything but the kitchen sink into the answer. The poor examiners had to work extremely hard to distil what we were really trying to say out of our answer. And we wondered why we didn't do so well when the results came out. Our friends who did brilliantly probably didn't write nearly so much but wrote what the examiner wanted to read – they answered the question.

There is a huge similarity between doing exams and making presentations – even apart from the nerves. Your audience has certain expectations when they come along to listen to you. They want to get something out of your presentation. You want to be successful so you must find out what that is.

Imagine you have been asked to make a presentation in two weeks' time. Your first task is to sit down quietly somewhere with a blank sheet of paper and a pen and write down your objectives for the presentation clearly.

Word to the Wise

If you start preparing a presentation with no particular objective in mind you can be fairly sure that you will finish it without achieving very much.

Ask yourself these questions to clarify your goal:

- Why am I making this presentation?
- What am I trying to achieve?
- What do I want to have in my audience's head as they leave the room?
- How do I want them to feel?
- What do I want them to do as a result of my presentation?

If you cannot answer these questions, then go back to the person who briefed you and ask them to clarify your purpose. You will make a much more effective presentation when you know first what your outcome needs to be.

About ten years ago I was responsible for selling a series of products. They were products which needed to be sold nationwide and in large volume. I decided that as I was good at making sales presentations, I would do my selling that way. It would get me to a large market relatively easily. I invited a large group of HR and training managers who were my potential customers to attend my first presentation and worked out what I was going to say to them. I was surprised at the numbers of people who were interested in attending and delighted at the interest they appeared to show on the night. However, I was disappointed by the number of sales. I knew I had made a good presentation, so why weren't they all queuing up to buy from me? It didn't make sense until I realised that I had set an unrealistic objective. They were not the sort of products you could sell en masse. HR and training managers needed time to make up their minds as to the suitability of the products; they also needed to talk through the relevance of the products to their own needs. I had to rethink my objectives for the presentation. I began to realise that although my overall objectives were still the same – to sell the products – the objectives for the actual presentation itself had to be different.

The new objectives that I set were:

- To raise awareness of the product
- To tell them that we were distributing this product
- To get them to agree to an appointment with me.

Not only were these objectives more realistic but by being very aware of them before I started putting the content together it meant that everything I said was leading the audience where I wanted them to go.

Who is your Target Audience?

Once you have set solid objectives, the next step is to think hard about your audience. There should be no such thing as a standard presentation that you deliver to every group of people. If your organisation has a standard presentation about the company that you deliver to each potential client, then you are losing out on a golden opportunity. Each presentation you make needs to be tailored for the specific audience you are talking to in order for it to be as effective as possible. Your presentation needs to be as much about your audience as you.

Word to the Wise

All presentations need to tailored to the specific audience they are aimed at in order to be effective.

Again, a set of questions:

- Who are your audience?
- How many of them will be there?
- What are their interests?
- What are they expecting to hear?
- What do they want to hear?
- Are they business people or not?
- If so, what levels are they at: more senior or more junior to me?
- Are they male or female?
- What age group are they?
- What profession are they in: accountants, solicitors, engineers, doctors?
- What functional areas do they work in: marketing, production, general management, IT, sales, finance?
- What are they measured on?
- What will excite them and get them thinking "this sounds interesting"?
- What do they know about this topic?
- How do they feel about this topic at the moment?
- What else is on their minds at the moment?

It sounds like a lot of questions but they will help you enormously when you are trying to connect with your audience. The best presentations are relevant to the audience because people will only really listen to a presenter if they think they are talking about something that is relevant to them. So the more homework you can do the better.

If you do not know enough about your audience, go back to the person who briefed you and find out. If you are going to talk to a potential customer, get on the internet and see what you can find out there. Ask around. What work have they done recently? What work do they specialise in? Have they upsized, downsized or remained static? Have they been in the newspapers recently, why? Get some history as well as current information. How long are they in business? Who founded the company? Is the founder still involved? Are they part of a multinational? If so, how big is the company worldwide? How important is the local operation? Will there be other nationalities at the presentation? If so, what language do they speak, other than English?

If you are speaking to a sports club, find out how they are doing recently, what competitors they have been up against and how they did, as well as how many teams, or equivalent, they have.

If you are talking to a group of employees in your own company, this research is just as important. You need to know what is currently at the forefront of their minds, what they are thinking about at the moment. Your topic may not be the most pressing matter in their minds; you need to tie your presentation in to their current problems and issues so that they feel you are worth listening to. At the very least you must know what is important to them.

All this information is vital in order to connect with your audience. If you can include facts and figures about the audience you are talking to they will be very impressed and feel flattered that you went to the trouble to find out about them. When people feel flattered, they tend to be impressed with their flatterer.

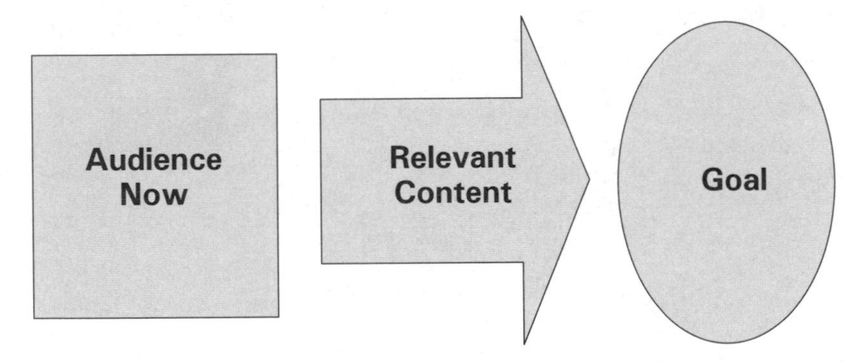

When you have worked out what your objectives are and done your homework on your audience, you can then start thinking about your content. Unfortunately, this is where most presenters start and they wonder why their audience goes to sleep.

The only content you should include in any presentation is that which will bring this particular audience towards the objective you have set for yourself. Anything else should be left out. Remember the exam question?

This is the most painful part, having to leave out information that you find interesting or that you spent hours, weeks or even months putting together. It may be interesting to you but if it is not going to interest your audience and bring them where you want to take them, it is waffle. Leave it out!

The Head and Heart Connection

We all like to believe we are rational, logical human beings. Some of you definitely are. However, most of us are only logical up to a point. Have you ever set yourself a limit for the amount you are going to spend on a particular item but when you are actually buying it, you end up spending nearly twice as much? Naturally, you justified the extra spending to yourself at the time: it will last longer than the cheaper one; it will save money over the long term; it is better quality; and other such reasons for spending next month's mortgage on it.

If you have, then you can be certain that something else is at work here. We have a tendency to make at least some of our decisions with our hearts, not our heads. We rationalise the decisions afterwards with facts and figures. If we really like something, all the logic seems to go out the window. If you make decisions this way, it is possible that your audience will engage in this type of behaviour too.

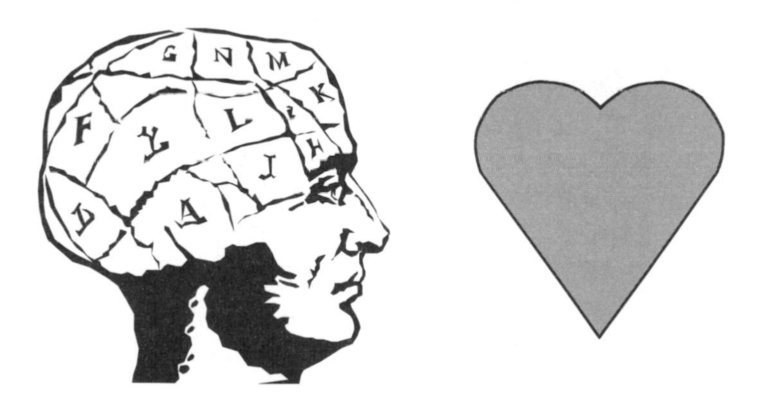

Therefore, when you want to get around them and persuade them to your way of thinking, you need to know as much about their wants, needs, desires and preferences as you can. Then make sure that you include these in your presentation. Of course you will have to back up your thoughts with facts and figures to give them enough ammunition to rationalise going along with you. When you get it right, they will be hooked.

Bringing it all Together

Collecting your content is a vital part of the process. When you know you have a presentation to make, maybe in a few weeks, take a big brown envelope or a manilla file, put the name of the presentation on it and leave it on the corner of your desk where you will see it every day. Every time you have an idea for content or find out anything about your target audience, scribble it down and put it in the envelope. Most of us have no problem having good ideas but when we are trying to pull them into shape, we often forget them. If you have captured them all in the same place you will find it easier to arrange them later.

You may have noticed that you don't have your best ideas when you are sitting at your desk. Most of us don't, unless we work in a very creative environment. We all have ideas in different places. If you do not know your most creative places, you should find out. Some typical ones are out walking the dog, digging the garden, in the loo, driving the car, lying in bed or in the shower. You will notice a common denominator in all these. It is hard to capture the ideas. That is one of the reasons you can be so creative. You are not trying to have an idea. You are busy doing something you enjoy, something relaxing. You need to discover your best ideas place and work out a way of capturing those ideas.

Try carrying around a small hardbacked notebook and pen, a dictaphone or a mobile phone. I have tried them all and they all work. The mobile phone is great at weekends: when an idea hits me, I ring my office voicemail and leave a message for myself for Monday morning. When I get to the office, I simply listen to my message (I know its horrible listening to a message from yourself, but if it works for you, you will get over it!), jot it down on a piece of paper and put it into the envelope.

Arranging your Material

About a week before the big day, you should take your envelope full of relevant bits and pieces and start putting a shape on what you are going to say. Keep your objectives beside you while you are doing this so you don't go charging off in the wrong direction. You must stay focused.

There is no standard way to arrange an effective presentation. It will depend entirely on your individual style, your audience and what you are trying to achieve. There are, however, some tips in Chapter 5 for capturing and holding attention which you should bear in mind when putting it all together.

You will have to decide at this stage how you will remember what you are going to say. I would advise strongly against reading from a written script. It is very hard to hold the attention of your audience in this way unless you have a professional script writer. The audience does not see enough of you. You cannot look at them, you are static and your script is rigid.

A much better way of going about it is to have a series of headings and sub-headings that you will talk around. Rehearse what you are going to say for each section but do not rely on it all being written down in front of you.

Sample notes for twenty-minute presentation

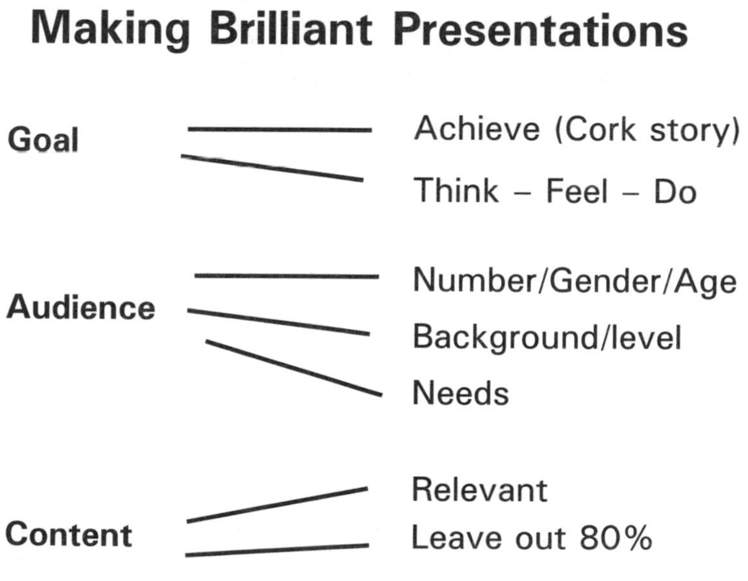

Making Brilliant Presentations

Goal — Achieve (Cork story)
— Think – Feel – Do

Audience — Number/Gender/Age
— Background/level
— Needs

Content — Relevant
— Leave out 80%

Another problem of writing out a full speech is that we write in written English but speak in conversational English. Written English tends to be more formal and uses longer words and sentences. This is more difficult for an audience to listen to and usually sounds contrived. If you want to write out your full script, translate it into conversational English afterwards and then go through it with a highlighter pen and underline the key points. This will help you to shape your thoughts as well as remember what you are going to say.

Rehearse, Rehearse, Rehearse!

All good presenters rehearse. I know you will feel a proper wally standing in front of the mirror talking away to yourself but if you have gone through what you are going to say a few times in advance, it will help you enormously with your delivery. If you watch any really good presenter, they make it sound as though they are having ideas off the top of their heads and thinking about how to get them across as they are saying them. Don't be fooled: this is not usually the case. Those really good presenters have probably rehearsed all those ad libs repeatedly until they sound just right.

You can rehearse wherever you like but you should try to have at least one rehearsal using all of the notes and audio-visual aids that you will be using on the day. For informal presentations, particularly regular ones that do not make you too nervous, this will probably be enough. If, however, you are making a formal, once-off presentation to a large group of people, you would be better to try to rehearse in the conference room or hall where you will be performing as well. You will need to work out where to stand, where to put your notes so you will be able to see them clearly and how you are going to get on and off the stage easily.

The reason I mention this point especially is that this is where I came unstuck when speaking at a large conference many years ago. I had even gone along to rehearse with the other speakers the night before bringing my slides and notes. The rehearsal had gone well, very well in fact. I felt good – nervous but confident – the next morning when I turned up in my glad rags, all ready for my big moment. Although I had meticulously rehearsed my content the night before, I had not thought about how to get on and off the podium. I know it sounds silly, but the night before I was wearing jeans and runners. Now I was in a tight skirt and shoes with a heel. All the rest of the speakers were men with long legs. Anyone who knows me will know that I am not a tall person. I was doing fine until I tried to step delicately onto the podium and realised that there was no step – this was no problem in jeans, but turned out to be a major problem in a tight skirt. Try as I might I could not get up, so there was nothing else for it but to hoist up the skirt and jump – in front of 200 people. That would have been okay except that as I was jumping I could hear a ripping noise: the seam at the back of my skirt had started to part company. All through my presentation, the only thing I could think of was how was I going to get back down to my seat without the entire audience seeing my ripped skirt. The moral of this story is that you should rehearse every aspect of your presentation. Try to cater for every eventuality and you will find that fewer things will go wrong.

Michael Colgrass explains an interesting way to rehearse in his book *My Lessons with Kumi: How I Learned to Perform with Confidence in Life and Work*. He suggests you take the position of three different people in order to give yourself feedback. You start by placing three pieces of

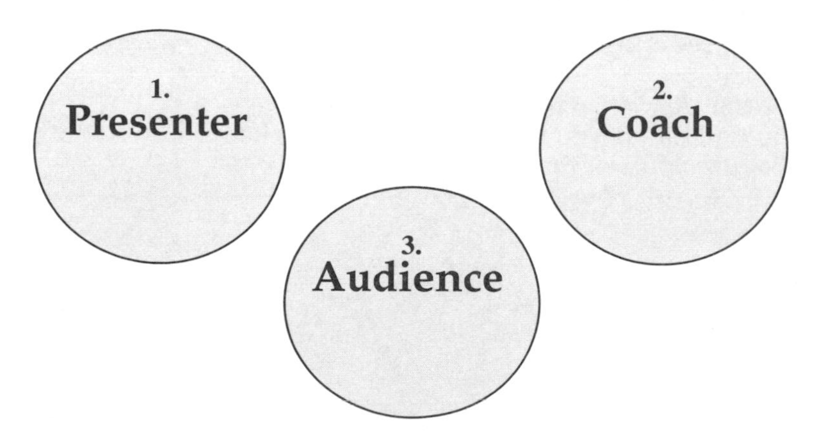

paper on the floor that represent the presenter (position one), the coach (position two) and the audience (position three). Mark them 1, 2 and 3 so you can tell one from the other.

1. **The Presenter:** Step into this first position and rehearse your presentation.
2. **The Coach:** Think of the person you would most like to have coach you for this presentation. See them standing in position two. Step out of performer mode and into coach mode. Become the coach. Tell your presenter what changes you would like them to make. Then step back to presenter mode and apply the advice. Shift between the two positions until you and your coach are satisfied with your presentation.
3. **The Audience:** Step into position three and watch and listen to the presentation from this position as the audience member. Tell the presenter what you would like to hear and see done differently. When you have all the advice from the audience member, step back into presenter position one and apply the feedback for the audience. Move between all three positions until you are satisfied.

This sounds like strange advice but it is a powerful way to give yourself feedback. You will notice the different feedback that the coach and disinterested observer give. The coach cares more about how you come across. The observer is much more casual. Both types of feedback are useful to get a rounded impression.

Do's and Don'ts

Don't include topics in your presentation that won't interest your audience
Don't set unrealistic objectives

Do set clear objectives before you start
Do find out all you can about your audience
Do give yourself time to rehearse

CHAPTER FOUR

The First 30 Seconds

This chapter will help you to:

- Manage your emotional state before you present
- Learn how to breathe well
- Make the most of the body-brain connection
- Use positive thoughts to enhance your delivery.

It is not just what you say that matters; it is also the way you say it. We will explore in subsequent chapters more about voice tone and body language but for now we will look at the last-minute preparation you need to do in order to make a brilliant first impression.

Most people find it difficult to start presentations. We are usually fine once we get started but the most difficult time for most of us is the ten minutes before we start and the first few minutes before we settle down. Luckily there are a few techniques you can use to help with this problem.

Managing your Emotional State

Firstly, you need to decide what emotional state you would like to be in when you are presenting. This will depend on the audience, the mood of the presentation and the message you are going to get across. Do you want this to be an up-beat presentation where you feel confident, relaxed and in control? Or would a more solemn, gentle and caring mood be more suitable? Are you trying to make them enthusiastic about buying your idea or product or are you trying to make them comfortable with a large expenditure you have just made?

> ***Word to the Wise***
>
> Your own emotional state will impact on your audience – so make sure you are in control of your own mood.

The emotional state you are in is contagious so it is vital to manage it carefully. Try this next exercise to help you to manage your emotional state before a presentation.

Brilliance Squared

1. Think of a time when you would like to present brilliantly.
2. Choose a positive state you would like to feel in that situation, e.g. confident or comfortable.
3. Think of a time you felt this state strongly, it can be from any time in your life. Pick a particular moment when this state was really strong.
4. Imagine a square in front of you; fill it with your favourite colour and imagine yourself standing in the square.
5. Close your eyes and step into your imaginary self in the square.
6. See what you saw, hear what you heard and feel what you felt the time you experienced your really strong, positive state (from step 3).
7. Intensify the state as the colour of the square gets stronger and immerses you.
8. Step out of your square and think of something else, i.e. break the state.
9. Imagine yourself actually making the presentation (from step 1) and step into your square.
10. Notice how much better you feel as you go through the same experience with the new feelings of excellence.

Once you have created this square for yourself, you will always have it. So before any presentation, just imagine your coloured square in front of you, step into it and feel the positive state flow through you.

Talking to Yourself

What you say to yourself is a large part of where your confidence comes from. We all have inner voices that say things to us constantly. Sometimes we can be negative: for instance, when we have a presentation coming up, we might say to ourselves, “I’m no good at presentations”, “I’m going to bore them to tears” or even “I’ll never get through this – they’ll

hate me". If we allow these negative messages to take root, they can adversely affect our ability to present. You may have come across the idea of the "self-fulfilling prophecy". This is where you say something to yourself so often that you will it to happen. "I'm going to trip as I walk up", "I'll forget my opening line". If you say these often enough, you will actually make it happen. You need to get rid of these niggling negative voices. Whenever you hear one of your negative voices, say firmly to it, "Shut the hell up!!!" Obviously you do not say this out loud or you will have other problems to deal with, but you can say it to your inner voice and it will stop bugging you.

The good news is that you can say positive things instead to replace those negative voices. When you do this, you encourage good things to happen.

Instead of:	Try:
I'm no good at presenting	I'm getting better at presenting each time
I'll bore them to tears	I've made it interesting so they will enjoy it
I'll never get through it	I've prepared well; they'll get a lot out of it
I'll trip on the way up	The last time I tripped; this time I'll be careful not to
I'll forget my opening line	I have my opening line ready – that'll grab them!

When you use these positive statements to yourself, you will be amazed at the difference it makes to your confidence level and the way you perform.

Learning to Breathe

Try this for a moment. Stand up and think of a situation that you are afraid of or that causes you anxiety when you think about it. Making your next presentation in a hostile environment would be ideal. Now notice your breathing. Is it deep and relaxed? The likelihood is that it is in fact constricted and shallow. Most people report that they are either hardly breathing at all or they stop altogether. This is quite natural: animals and humans freeze at the possibility of danger – they stop breathing so they can hear better. This carries through for when we are in a stressful or fearful situation like presenting. We tend to tense up and reduce our breathing. As we saw in Chapter 1, our body responds to imagined danger the same way as if it were real.

Try standing up again, close your eyes and take a few slow, even, deep breaths. Imagine the breath is going deep into your body, deeper with each in-breath. Notice how you are feeling now. It is likely that there is less tension in your body now and your mind is more at ease. Tension and deep breathing do not mix. If you are stressed, your breathing is likely to be shallow. However, you can change this by breathing deeply and making your body and mind relax. You can therefore train yourself to be more relaxed when faced with stressful situations, such as presenting.

> ***Word to the Wise***
>
> When you get nervous, you get out of breath fast. Learn how to control your breathing so you can stay in control of your delivery.

Most people do not know how it feels to take a full breath. Observe others while they are breathing and you will notice that their breath gets drawn in quite quickly, raising their shoulders. This is a high hard breath, not a full one. Only the tops of the lungs get filled and the shoulders get moved up into a tense position.

A deep breath is much more beneficial. This is where you inhale deeply into your torso, filling your lungs right to the bottom, pushing out your stomach. Better again is what Dr Joseph Parent describes as a full breath in *Zen Golf: Mastering the Mental Game*. Try sitting or standing with good posture and close your eyes. Breathe gently and slowly through your nose. Find the breath going down the back of your throat. On the next few breaths, feel as if your breath were going into your back, filling it first from side to side, then down to the base of your spine. As you breathe this way, you will feel your shoulder blades widen a little and the back of your rib cage spread wider. Finally, your back will seem to get longer as you feel as though the breath is reaching down to the base of your spine. Practice this way of breathing every day. Soon it will become your natural way of breathing. Making full use of your lungs is hugely beneficial. This way, you are providing the maximum amount of oxygen to your blood and through it to your muscles and your brain, which helps you to think more clearly.

Now try something else. Just stand up! Go on, stand up now. Notice what you did with your breathing as you stood. Most of us naturally breathe in as we stand up. This can leave us breathless just as we open our mouths to speak which can lead us to shallow breathing while we're presenting. If you have ever worked out in a gym, you will know that as you lift the weight or execute the push part of an exercise, you should breathe out. It is the same with presenting: just before you stand up, take a deep breath in and then stand up on an out-breath.

The Eyes have It!

There are three different representational systems: visual, hearing and feeling (see Chapter 5 for full explanation). While we are working on these different systems or channels, we move our eyes in different directions to help our brains to access different types of information.

For instance, have you ever sat in a maths exam, trying to picture a formula in your head? You looked at it in the text book last night. You nearly have it … Got it! Where were your eyes while you were trying to picture that formula? It is likely they were looking up towards the ceiling, either to the left if you were simply remembering it, or to the right, if you were constructing it. This is where our visual memory is stored.

What about when someone asks you to remember the words of a song you know or to recall the exact words that were said at a meeting yesterday? Where do your eyes go now? It is usual to look to the side for this type of information. Again, either to the left to recall it or to the right, to construct it.

When you are talking to yourself, you are most probably looking down to the left.

The last position is when you are accessing your feelings. When you are thinking, "This doesn't feel too good" or "I'm exhausted", your eyes are usually looking down to the right. See the diagram overleaf for a visual representation of all six positions.

These positions will be correct for most people. However, those who are left-handed and some others will sometimes be switched the other way around.

Now that you know where your eyes are when you are looking for different types of information, you can use this to your advantage when you are about to present. It is worth observing different presenters just before and just as they start speaking. See where their eyes are and see what impact it has on their own state and on the audience.

Presenters often walk up to start, drop their eyes to the floor, then start their presentation. What they are most probably doing is accessing their feelings – "I feel sick" – or listening to their inner voice – "I hate presenting, I'm going to bore them to tears again". Just imagine what that is doing to their emotional state while this is happening. And what do the audience see? Maybe they see discomfort and fear. They certainly do not see confidence or joy.

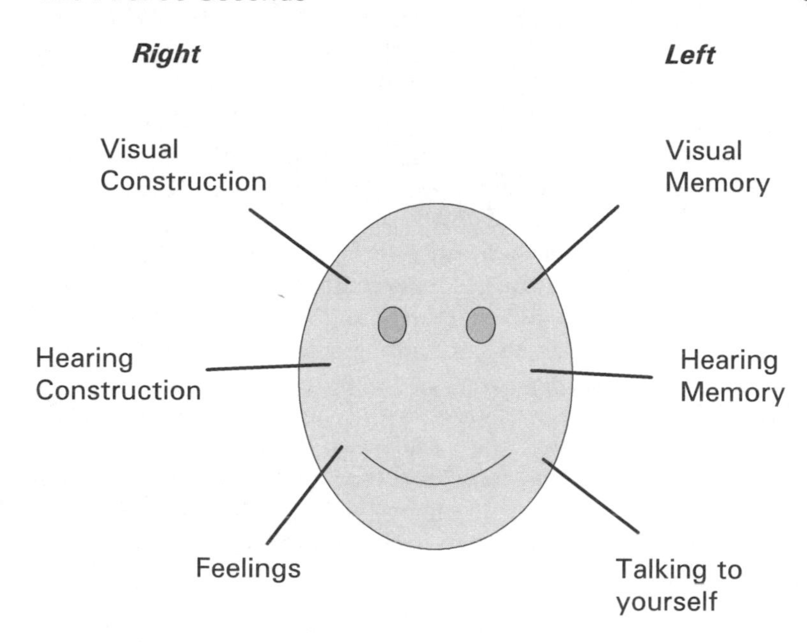

This diagram is as you are looking at someone else

Another way that presenters can start is to look up at the ceiling before they say their opening line. Here they are probably searching for what they are going to say. Because they are not looking at the audience, they are losing that connection which is vital at the early stages and the audience may see uncertainty and lack of knowledge.

The main issue to be aware of here is that there is a difference between what Michael Colgrass calls your private state and your public state. Particularly if you are nervous, you don't want to bring this private state on with you and let it be seen publicly. You need to handle the transition carefully. While you are still sitting, or standing ready to be introduced, you need to prepare yourself. Think about your opening line. Decide how you are going to walk on and where you will leave your notes. Then take a deep breath – this will act as the division between what you were doing (waiting and preparing) and what you are about to do (connect with your audience and present). Breathe out as you stand up, start getting eye contact with your audience – or if you have to walk a good distance, look straight ahead – don't let your eyes drop to the floor or wander up to the ceiling. Hold them at this level while you arrive in front of your audience. Pause when you have arrived. Connect with their eyes. Then deliver your opening line.

The Body-Brain Connection

Your physiology or body position has a huge impact on your brain or your mood. Take a moment to try this out. Slump down in your chair with a long face. How does that position make you feel? Usually, this can make us feel lethargic, lack lustre and a little depressed. Now try standing up straight with a smile on your face. Now you probably feel happier, more enthusiastic and generally sharper. Notice the difference?

If you want to feel confident, relaxed and focused, make sure your body position reflects this. Practice sitting, standing and walking in a confident way and become aware of the difference it makes to your mood. Presenters who enter the room with a confident walk actually give the impression that they know what they are doing, are knowledgeable and therefore have more credibility than those who look stressed, uncomfortable and with sagging body posture. You will notice too that simply walking confidently will make you feel confident.

Centre of Gravity

Another connection that is not well known is that of our state of mind and our centre of gravity. Wherever our mind is focused, the centre of gravity will shift in that direction. When you are uptight, worried, thinking about what you are going to say, your centre of gravity will be up near to your head. But when you feel grounded, down-to-earth and confident, your centre of gravity will move down to your body centre and you will be steadier on your feet. Have you ever watched a presenter who is "all over the place"? They seem to sway and wobble a lot. They shift from foot to foot and appear uncomfortable. They are sometimes quite difficult to watch as they can make you feel uncomfortable.

A comfortable presenter appears well-grounded, comfortable and each movement looks like it is deliberate. This presenter will have more credibility than the first but will also enjoy presenting more as they will be feeling more in control. Try this exercise with a partner. Stand upright, with feet shoulder width apart and knees slightly bent (not locked). Close your eyes and focus your attention on your chest and upper back and feel as if most of the weight of your body is there in your upper torso. As you breathe out, feel that the weight is settling lower in your body, at the level of your ribs. With the next breath, feel it settling down in your stomach. With the next breath, feel it a few inches below your belly button. You will feel that most of the weight of your body is centred just below your belly button. Now, ask your partner to hold your arm and push lightly against your shoulder. You will feel your shoulder give a bit, but your lower body remains stable.

Do this again, taking the same position, but this time put your attention on your forehead, clench your jaw and tense the muscles where your shoulders meet your neck. Feel that most of your weight is there on your shoulders, neck and head. Now move it up even higher – until it is about a foot above your head. Again, ask your partner to give you a little push in the same place, making sure that they are holding your arm. It is quite likely that the same push that had little effect on you the last time will make you take a step back to keep your balance.

Obviously, nothing physically changed in the actual weight distribution in your body, but there was a clear physical difference based on the change in your centre of gravity created by your mind. In the Japanese martial arts your centre of gravity is called the "hara"; in the Chinese traditions such as Tai Chi it is called the "dantien"; and in Tibetan Yoga it is called the "chojung".

Do's and Don'ts

Don't allow your emotional state to upset your audience
Don't listen to your negative voices
Don't forget to breathe

Do manage your own emotional state – it is contagious
Do say positive things to yourself – remember your previous successes
Do learn to breathe well
Do become aware of the direction of your eyes and what effect it is having on you and your audience
Do find and use your centre of gravity – it will give you confidence

CHAPTER FIVE

Grabbing and Holding Attention

This chapter will help you to:

- Grab the attention of your audience
- Make your presentation relevant to each of them
- Make your audience remember your key points.

The first minute of any presentation is when the audience will decide whether you are worth listening to. So you have to make an impact during this first minute or you will lose them. Presenters who start limply with, "Hello, my name is Joe Bloggs and I'm here to talk to you about …" are likely to lose their audience before they even begin their presentation. They are not saying anything that will attract the audience's attention. They are not waking them up. They sound boring.

Equally important is the end of your presentation. You will often hear speakers finishing with an innocuous line such as, "Well, that's all I have to tell you about that, I think that's it". How exciting!! How absolutely riveting!!! The problem is that the audience will remember most of what was said during the last minute, particularly if the speaker has said one of the key finishing phrases a minute from the end such as "And finally …", "And just to summarise …", "To pull it all together …", "In conclusion …". Have you ever noticed how an audience reacts when one of these phrases is used? Everyone sits up and starts to get interested again. All the people who were asleep or thinking about other more important issues will suddenly straighten up in their chairs and listen for the next minute. Don't waste this minute. You have everyone's undivided attention. Make the most of it.

What I have been describing above are two psychological phenomena called "primacy" and "recency". We tend to remember most about the first thing that happens and the last thing that happens. To illustrate this point, let me give you two examples.

Take a situation you may be in socially. You have decided to go to a restaurant on a Saturday night. It is a restaurant you have been to once before about six months ago. You know it is a lovely place and the food was good last time so you feel confident that you and your partner will enjoy the evening. You reserve a table for 8.00 p.m. You arrive on time. As you are standing by the door, the head waiter seems to look straight through you. You are not getting much attention. In fact nobody has even come near you. You begin to feel embarrassed but realise that he is busy so you wait patiently. After a few minutes of being ignored, the door opens again and another couple come in behind you. The head waiter sees them immediately and waves them into the restaurant with a big smile, leaving you standing by the door. Finally, after another few minutes, he comes over to you with a strained face and says coolly, "Follow me," and shows you to a table beside the door to the gents toilets. By now you are feeling pretty bad about the restaurant and are likely to be looking for any fault you can find to complain about. If there is a stain on the table cloth, you will notice it; if the service is slow, you will get angry; if the food is cold or not well cooked, you will be livid. In other words, if the start of a service encounter is not good, you will be looking for more problems.

What about the opposite situation. You arrive at the same restaurant and as you come in through the door, the head waiter is immediately over to you, welcoming you like a long lost friend. "Good evening, it's lovely to see you again," he says as he shows you to a lovely table just beside the window. Now you have been made to feel a little special. If there is a stain on the table cloth, you are likely to put the salt cellar on top of it rather than complain about it; you will hardly notice if the service is slow; and if the meal isn't the best you may decide that you come here for the atmosphere, not the food.

You may at some time have been involved in recruitment interviewing. If you are interviewing a few people for the same job, you will have noticed that as you interview the first one you pay a lot of attention to them. They are the first one, after all. You are fresh. The second candidate comes in through the door and you immediately start measuring them against the previous candidate. The third and fourth candidates appear and you do the same, always measuring against the first candidate. The last person comes along and because they are the last and final candidate you start paying attention again. You may also notice that when you are sitting down after all the interviewees are gone, you can remember most about the first and last candidates. This is the effect of the primacy and recency effect. If all else is equal, the first or last candidate stand the best chance of getting the job. The first candidate sets the standard against which all the others will be measured and you will be able to remember most about the last one because they were the most recent.

The same principles apply to presentations. If you really want to make an impact on your audience you need to pay particular attention to the start and end of your presentation.

> ***Word to the Wise***
> Always open and close your presentation with a bang.

Start with a Bang

What this means is simply thinking about your audience and making sure that you start with something they will be interested in. Try telling them something they don't already know. Give them an interesting statistic, ask them a question, tell them a story. Above all, talk to them about something that is uppermost in their mind. Remember, this is the point where they are deciding whether they will stay awake and listen to you or not. Make it worth their while to stay with you. Make it sound as though they cannot possibly miss your presentation. Make it exciting.

Add a Memorable Ending

You need to remind your audience what you have been talking about within the last few minutes. Then give them something definite to think

about or do as a result of what you have been saying. Your last sentence should reflect your objectives. This is what is going to be in your audience's head as they leave.

Communicating Effectively

But what about the body of the presentation? How do you make that interesting? Have you ever talked to a colleague and decided that you would both like to attend a talk some afternoon but only one of you can. Your colleague goes along. You meet that evening and ask her how the presentation went. She says it was great, very interesting, pity you had not been able to go as well. However, when you ask her what the speaker said, she cannot remember anything. This often happens; the presenter entertains but their points are not memorable. How can you make sure that your audience will remember what you have said? For a start you must make it relevant to them but you must also try to think about the way they are communicating.

Three Communication Channels

According to Richard Bandler and John Grinder, we all work on three different communication channels. These are visual, auditory and kinesthetic. John Townsend simplified the language and gave us an easier way to remember them:

Use *all* Communication channels

Visual

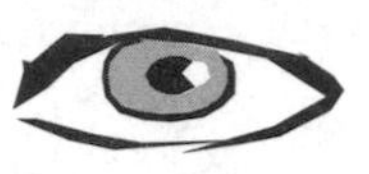

Hearing

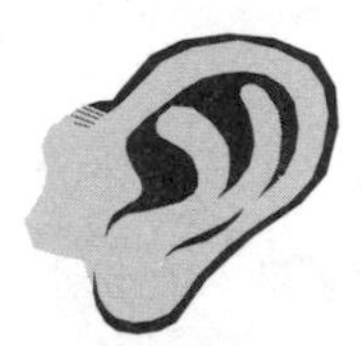

Feeling

All of us use all three to communicate but most of us have a preferred channel that we use more easily and regularly. Take, for instance, a situation where a friend asks you for directions to your house. How are you likely to give those directions? A visual person will draw a map – it may not be a great map but at least it is visual. A hearing person will give specific directions – first right, second left, right at the T junction and fourth turn on the left. A person working on the feeling channel as a preference will be more likely to say things like, "Remember that pub we had a pint in last week, the one on the corner? Well turn right there. Then you go to the church where Pat and Sheila got married and turn left there. Then its right at the T junction where the green is in front of you."

If you listen to different people speaking, you will notice that we use quite different words and phrases to express ourselves.

Visual phrases
I see what you mean
We are going to have to look closely at this idea
Why don't I look into this and get back to you?
What are your views on this?
I cannot quite visualise how it will work
Let's take a helicopter view of this
The picture is a little fuzzy – I need more clarity about this

Hearing phrases
I hear what you are saying
I don't like the sound of this
That went in one ear and out the other
That rings a bell
That's music to my ears
Sounds like a great idea, tell me more about it!

Feeling phrases
I will be in touch with you soon
I have a gut feeling about this
This doesn't feel right to me
I can't put my finger on what's wrong
We have to get to grips with this problem
Sucking information out of that crowd is like pulling teeth

We all use these phrases from time to time but if you find yourself using one type rather than the others, then it will give you a good idea which communication channel is your preference. Your audience will be made up of a mixture of people with the different preferences. To really grab the attention of each of them you need to ensure you are explaining each point in three different ways. This will also mean that each audience member will get each key point three times. This will help them to remember your all important messages.

For further evidence of this, Edgar Dale, a researcher, developed what is now known as "Dale's Cone of Experience".

He says people will remember:
20 per cent of what they hear
30 per cent of what they see
50 per cent of what they see and hear
80 per cent of what they hear, see and do

There is another group of people who tend not to use sensory information or phrases at all. You could call this group "neutrals". Their preference is for data, statistics, logical arguments, facts and figures. They are not so interested in the "fluffy stuff". The key phrases they tend to use are:

Neutral phrases
Statistically speaking, this doesn't add up
This seems reasonable
I understand your issue
I know about this type of problem
The logic of this idea is fine with me

To ensure you get the message across to everyone in your audience, you must connect with all channels. So, for each key point, try to get your message across, using evidence, key facts and figures and logical arguments (neutrals). Show them what you mean by using visuals, props, illustrations, photographs, graphs and charts (visuals). Then use sounds, music – tell them stories, being aware of using different voice tones and pay particular attention to language (hearing). Finally, make sure to give them examples to help them feel how they could use the information you are giving them, help them feel the emotions of a situation or the consequences of not making a target. Try asking them questions; encourage audience participation in some way. If you can get them involved by working through a real example, it will be even more powerful (feelings).

Word to the Wise

Make your presentation and all your key points relevant to your audience.

Make it Relevant

Your audience will be most interested in the parts of your presentation that are directly relevant to them. You may have noticed what encourages you to listen: usually anything that has an impact on your life, your job, your family, your earnings, your future -- in fact any issue of importance to you.

Talk directly to your audience. Do not put them in the third party, this will make them think you are talking to someone else and it will lose its relevance. For example, if you are trying to motivate a group of salespeople, don't say, "The salespeople are going to have to really push the boat out this next quarter if the company targets are going to be met." This is too impersonal. Try instead, "We are relying on you to make the difference. You are the ones out there talking to the customers – you know the business. If you can push the boat out for the next quarter, we can reach our targets and we'll all do well at the end of the year." This is much more personal. Note the use of the word "you". This is one of the most powerful words in the English language. It makes what you are saying appear relevant to the audience. It makes them sit up and take notice.

Keep the Number of Points Small

If you try to get too many points across at one time, you run the risk of your audience forgetting them all. Imagine you are just nipping down to the local shops to buy a few things you have run short on during the week. You need bread, milk and cat food. Those three things are relatively easy to remember between here and the shops. But what happens when you are asked to remember a fourth or fifth item? Unless you are blessed with a good memory, it suddenly seems like a mammoth task to memorise them all the way to the shops. The more you try to remember the more likely you are to forget all of the needed items.

Do not expect your audience to remember any more than five points; it is even better if you can keep it down to three.

The Power of Threes

Have you ever noticed how often things in life happen in threes?

- Morning, noon and night
- Faith, hope and charity
- The Father, Son and Holy Ghost
- This, that and the other
- The sun, moon and stars
- Tom, Dick and Harry
- The good, the bad and the ugly

There is a great rhythm in threes. They add a lot of interest to a presentation when you use them – they add punch, colour and "oomph!" to your speech.

Acronyms as Memory Aids

Acronyms can be a powerful memory tool – not just for the audience, but for you too. They work best when they have real meaning, like the VHF explained earlier in this chapter. John Townsend talks about three channels; VHF is a channel. This helps to make it memorable for a long time. It is essential that each letter represents the key thought in the concept you want them to remember. One that I find works well when teaching presentation skills is this:

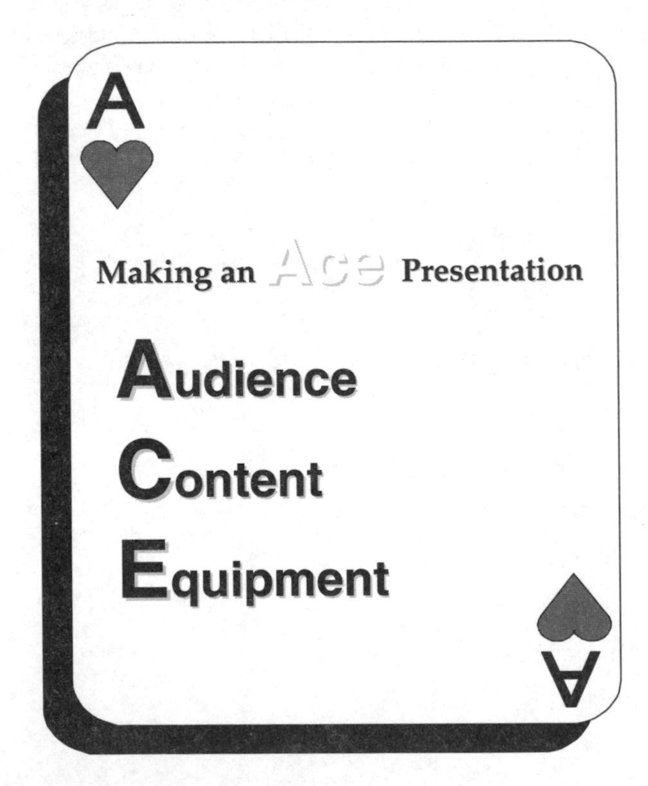

Each key concept is represented in the word ACE. It has the added advantage in that there is a strong visual possibility.

Analogies

Some years ago, I asked a group of participants on one of my courses to make a presentation on "The Elements of a Good Presentation". They put together a wonderful presentation using the analogy of building a fire.

> "To start a fire, you need a spark; so too with a presentation, you need an opening bang.
>
> A fire needs three or four main logs or briquettes as a framework; a presentation must have three or four key points or concepts.
>
> In between these main logs are smaller sticks or newspaper; in the case of a presentation, these are the stories, examples and sub-points.
>
> The overall feeling you get when you sit in front of a good fire is a warm glow; this should be how you feel when you watch a good presentation."

The participants brought the analogy to life through a step-by-step visual build up of the fire, using overhead overlays. It was superb and unforgettable.

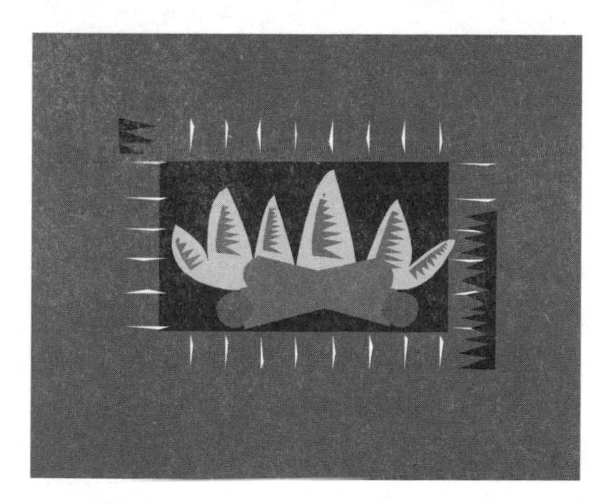

Analogies can be drawn from all walks of life; sporting analogies can be particularly powerful. Just make sure your audience has an interest in the analogy you have thought of, otherwise you run the risk of making your points even less digestible.

Do's and Don'ts

Don't try to tell your audience too much
Don't start and finish limply
Don't talk to your audience in the third party

Do use all three communication channels
Do make everything relevant to your audience
Do use analogies, stories and acronyms as memory aids

CHAPTER SIX

Influencing and Persuading

This chapter will help you to:

- Understand that you are selling
- Turn features into benefits
- Use a framework to influence your audience
- Use the best words to sell.

I remember working with a hotel some years ago. It was a very successful hotel with a strong reputation for customer service. It had been having a problem in the previous few months with reservations staff. They were a nice bunch of people who dealt with customer enquiries in a friendly and courteous manner. The problem was that for some time they had not been turning enough of these enquiries into sales.

I spent some time listening to the team in action. What they were doing was selling the features of the hotel, not the benefits and to make matters worse, they were selling all the features to all of the customers. In the last chapter, we looked at the importance of relevance. They were breaking this rule blatantly. Features of the hotel included a leisure centre with water slide, jacuzzi and steam room; a variety of restaurants; a bar with live music; all rooms en suite with TV and telephone and lots more.

When a hotel is described as above it sounds sterile and impersonal. Details like this simply give you information; they do not persuade you to buy. If you are to be excited by this hotel, you need to hear what it can do for *you*. The benefits actually tell you what the features can do for you, thereby making them more personal and relevant. A presentation must do the same.

You may be saying to yourself at this point, "But I don't make sales presentations!" Are you sure? When I ask course participants what types of presentations they make, they often tell me that they are only there to give information. I don't really believe that. Whenever you stand up in front of a group of people you are always trying to sell something. It may be your company, a product or service or an idea; and if you are not selling any of these you are certainly selling yourself.

Most presentations are about selling. You are trying to move your audience from one point of view to another. When you are talking to a group of employees in your department about the last three months' results, what are you really trying to do? You are hoping to encourage them to work as hard or even harder for the next quarter, or you certainly should be. If you are a department head talking to the senior management team about what your department has been doing over the past month, you are not just giving information; you are selling your department and its hard-working staff to the management team.

> ***Word to the Wise***
>
> Whatever else you are trying to do in a presentation, you are always selling something.

Whatever else you are doing, you are always selling something. Remember the objectives in Chapter 3? Be clear about exactly what you are hoping to achieve before you start. Do you want to move your audience from one point of view to another? To achieve even a subtle change you need to influence and persuade. What influences you to buy, or to change your mind? For most people it is usually when they feel there is some advantage for them in changing their way of thinking. You must try to show the audience that changing their way of thinking is to their benefit; otherwise, they may not bother.

Selling Benefits to your Audience

Let's look at some examples of features, advantages and benefits.

> **Features**
>
> Features are neutral facts, data, information or characteristics that describe what you are selling. For example:
>
> - It will cost €10,000
> - There is a 3-year warranty
> - We have 15 branch offices, nation-wide

These do not tend to have much impact on a potential buyer. They are too impersonal, too distant and do not easily fit the needs of the audience.

Advantages
Advantages show how products, services or your idea can be used. For example:

- … which means it is easy to use
- … so it is the quietest on the market
- … which means it can be used in any country

Average salespeople use advantages to sell. They let you go a step further than features and put what you are selling into context for your audience.

Word to the Wise

Real benefits of your product, service or idea are much more persuasive than features and advantages.

Benefits
Benefits show how what you are selling meets an explicit need of your audience. For example:

- So you will have higher profits
- So you will be able to get things done quickly
- So it will be easier for you to get to …

The best salespeople use benefits. This is why, more than anything else, you need to know your audience and their needs. If you do not know what your audience wants, you will not know what benefits to sell.

Take the hotel example above. The features of a hotel may be:

- leisure centre with jacuzzi, steam room and beauty salon
- supervised children's playroom
- romantic dining room
- baby listening service
- beside theatres and cinemas
- luxurious bedrooms with king-size, four-poster beds
- family rooms

but these will not sell the hotel by themselves. If you were aware of the advantages of each of these, it could help you to decide.

Advantages could be:

- Baby listening service, family rooms and supervised children's playroom will keep children safe
- Because the hotel is beside theatres and cinemas there will be plenty of entertainment
- Romantic dining room and luxurious bedrooms will mean it is a place suitable for couples
- Leisure centre will provide entertainment for children and relaxation for adults.

They are still a little impersonal though. What will these advantages actually do for you? For a start, you will notice that some will help to sell a weekend away for a couple; others will help to sell a holiday to a family. You must work out who your audience is. If you are selling your hotel to one category of people, you should only sell the benefits that will influence that group.

For couples looking for a romantic weekend away, you could sell them:
A lovely, romantic setting with a cosy dining room and luxurious bedrooms with king-size four-poster beds so that *you* can get away from it all. *You* can relax and wind down in the leisure centre and soak the working week away in the jacuzzi and steam room. *You* will go home ready to face anything.

A family with children may be more concerned about the safety and entertainment of the children. But what is really important is what that will do for them.

For a couple who want to bring their children away with them, you could sell them:
Your children will be supervised by qualified, friendly staff in a state-of-the-art playroom so *you* can have peace of mind while *you* relax in the leisure centre or pamper *yourselves* in the beauty salon. There is a baby listening service so *you* can go out and enjoy *yourselves* at the local theatre without having to worry about the baby waking up.

In both cases you are selling relaxation but in two different ways. In order to persuade your audience you must make them *feel* the benefits, not just know them intellectually. The best presenters will have done their homework on the audience in advance and will be able to sell the benefits to satisfy the needs of any group within the audience. Notice the use of the word "you". All benefit statements must include this word for them to be most effective.

A Structured Approach to Influencing

This is a structure that works well for persuasive presentations. There are four simple steps:

1. Create Dissatisfaction

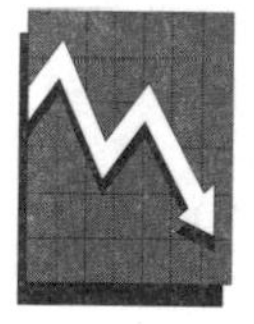

2. Paint bright future

3. Practical steps

4. Reduce risk

Imagine you are trying the sell the idea of a new telephone system, costing €20,000, for your company to senior management. First, work out your goal, then analyse your audience (see Chapter 3).

Set the Goal

Your overall goal is that you want agreement for the new system. However, it is unlikely you will get this in a ten-minute slot at a management meeting, especially if you know that you have some people in the audience who are hostile towards the idea. So what you are really looking for from this short presentation is agreement, in principle, for you to look further into the issue and bring back an in-depth report at a later meeting. This is much easier for them to say yes to, and you will have got them to make a small commitment towards your goal, which puts you at an advantage.

Know your Audience

There are six senior managers: the MD, who has a reputation for caring for his customers; the production manager, who recently came from a tough manufacturing environment where there were no frills (he thinks the MD is a bit soft and if the staff only worked a bit harder, there would be no problems with the telephone system – he is measured on productivity); the financial controller, whose main concern at the moment is cost-cutting; the IT manager, who loves technology of any sort, gadgets are her hobby; the sales and marketing manager, who is always on the road and has a team of twelve salespeople to contend with and seems to spend his life dealing with complaints from customers and reps because they all find it difficult to stay in touch with head office; and the human resources manager, who is worried about staff morale as they feel no one listens to them. The staff have been complaining about the quality of the telephone system for years.

Looking at the diverse group above, you can guess that three people will be reasonably supportive, i.e. the MD, the sales and marketing manager and the HR manager, but only if you show them that the new system will help them with their agendas of listening to the staff and helping them to contact customers more easily. The financial controller will be okay once you can show it will save and even make money for the company. The production manager's main concern is productivity so he must see that the system can help staff to work harder. The IT manager must see that the latest technology is being employed and needs to be involved in choosing the system. The overall thrust of a group at this level is also higher profitability and image in the marketplace.

This gives us a few themes to work with:

- The new system will show we are listening to staff and helping to increase sales and reduce complaints
- It will lead to higher productivity
- It will lead to cost savings, or at least will not cost much more, and any costs will be outweighed by gains in profitability
- It will improve our image in the marketplace.

Slotting this into the model:

1. Create Dissatisfaction with the Status Quo

- State number of lost calls through bad connections
- State number of lost calls through customers having to wait too long
- Talk about the number of dissatisfied customers because of the problems associated with the existing phone system
- Identify the frustrated feelings of staff from dealing with customers made angry by the phone system
- Mention that their management time is being wasted by angry customers, escalating their problems
- Describe how the image of the company is suffering due to poor service
- Show evidence that companies who provide excellent customer service retain more customers
- And that long-term customers are more profitable than short-term customers
- Point out how much profit to the company can be lost due to bad phone service

Notice that all these are based on fact, either researched within the company or outside. You will also see that some of the above facts will appeal to the "neutrals" in the audience, others will appeal to the "feelings people". All can be made accessible to the visual people through the clever use of charts and graphs and put across well in a suitable voice tone, with useful examples and stories for the "hearing people". What this stage of the model does is create a need for change.

2. Paint a Vision of a Bright Future

- Remind them that the company wants to make money – that is why they are here
- Get them to imagine a profitable company – share price rising, with bonuses for everyone
- Describe the company having high staff morale
- Say that happy customers will refer the company to their friends and colleagues
- Point out that there will be less frustration for them – less angry customers escalating their problems to senior management
- State that there will be more time for them to handle the real issues of the business
- Describe the possibility of the company having a dynamic, forward-looking image
- Get your audience to identify with a general feel-good factor in the company

These points are aimed specifically at the audience and will help them to remain interested and be influenced. This stage of the model convinces them to want to change.

It is usually necessary to give some sort of cost/benefit analysis when asking anyone to spend money. Companies will not agree to invest unless they can see that the benefits actually will outweigh the cost. This sounds obvious but often when we think something is a good idea we overlook the obvious and assume that our audience will see the benefits as clearly as we do. Never make this assumption. Benefits need to be laid out explicitly.

3. Set out easy, practical steps

- Ask them to agree on principle that a new phone system is a good idea at today's meeting
- Tell them that you will get three competitive quotes for the next meeting in a month's time
- Outline the decision criteria
- Tell them you would like to use the considerable experience of the IT manager to help you to identify the best system
- Tell them that all stationery will be printed with the new number(s) by the time the new system is installed
- Explain that the new system will be up and running in six months' time
- Make them aware that there will be follow-up training and monitoring

These steps must show how easy it will be to make this decision. Any ambiguity may hold up the decision. Try to think ahead to any objections your audience may have to your suggestion and counter them in advance.

4. Reduce the risk

- State that staff will receive comprehensive training so there will be no hitches or teething problems
- Mention that staff will give out direct dial numbers to all customers so there will be less traffic through the switchboard
- Talk about having a trial run during the least busy period
- Say that this system has been tried and tested by companies A, B, C and D
- Tell the audience that you will arrange an on-site engineer for the first two days to iron out any hitches in the system
- Promise to run parallel systems over the first six months
- Tell them that there will be payback within the first two years in saved customers
- Convince them that a new phone system will enable the company to get a better name in the marketplace

This structure can now be made into a very influential and persuasive presentation, adding a punchy start and a memorable ending, punctuated throughout with relevant examples.

Use Persuasive Words and Phrases

Your use of words can also be important. Use too much jargon or stuffy language and you are doomed to fail. There are some words and phrases that are more persuasive than others. Twelve words that have extraordinary persuasive power are:

You	***Easy***	***Guarantee***
Money	***Discovery***	***Results***
Love	***New***	***Proven***
Help	***Save***	***Free***

Source: Dept of Psychology, Yale University.

You will recognise all of these words from their regular use in advertising. This shows that they work. No company would waste advertising money using words that do not persuade.

The word "you" is probably the most persuasive of all. It connects what you are talking about directly to the listener and makes them believe it is relevant to them. Some opening phrases that can grab attention in a persuasive presentation:[1]

Questions
Did you ever ask yourself …?
Isn't it time you …?
Did you know that …?
Will you be ready for the …?
Wouldn't you like to …?

Statements
If you are like most people, you probably …
It's hard enough to … without having to worry about …
You have probably noticed that …
Just wait until you …

[1] Richard Bayan, *Words that Sell*, Contemporary Books, 1984.

Challenges
If you are seriously interested in …
Match yourself against …
Join the small handful of people who …
Let your imagination soar …

When you are trying to justify a high price during the presentation
Isn't it worth paying a little extra for …?
Not as expensive as you think
You probably thought you couldn't afford …

And some closing statements
This is the opportunity you have been waiting for
In short, you have nothing to lose
You will still be able to do it your way – only better!
Try to imagine the alternative

Try to avoid long, formal words or phrases when you could use short, easily understood ones. Unless you are speaking to an academic audience you want to speak in conversational English. Here are some words and phrases that make a presentation sound formal and inaccessible (left), with some simpler translations (right).

At this point in time	Now
Conceptualise	Think
Continuum	Link
Impact negatively	Worsen
Inoperative	Doesn't work
Interface	Meet, work with
Normalise	Return to normal
Optimal	Ideal
Overriding	Major
Pursuant to	According to
Ramifications	Consequences
Terminated	Finished
With reference to	About
Pertaining to	About
Owing to the fact that	Since
Reach a conclusion as to	Decide
Be cognisant of	Know
Is of the opinion	Believes
Make enquiry regarding	Enquire

All of these words are long-winded and need to be shortened so that your audience can stay in contact with you. You will never persuade your audience if they cannot easily understand the message you are trying to get across.

Positive versus Negative Words and Phrases

When we are trying to persuade, we will often fall into the trap of using negative phrases in the hope of steering our audience away from a negative thought. Some examples you will often hear are "This isn't as expensive as you think", "The costs won't be high", "This won't take up much of your time" or even "I hope I won't bore you but I need to give you some more details". When we hear any of these types of phrases, the negative thought can take root in our minds. For instance, what happens if I say to you "Don't think of a pink cat"?

What is the image that comes into your mind? I bet it's a pink cat. You need to re-phrase your negative phrases into positive ones. Instead of saying that it will not be expensive, try saying that it is good value or that the costs will be reasonable. This will be much more persuasive and will help you to keep positive thoughts in your audience's mind throughout your presentation.

Do's and Don'ts

Don't just sell features to an audience
Don't use big words where little ones would do
Don't put things into the third party – it makes them impersonal

Do remember that you are always selling something
Do sell benefits that fit the needs of your audience
Do use powerful, persuasive words in your presentations to sell
Do use a structured approach to influence your audience

CHAPTER SEVEN

Storytelling

This chapter will help you to:

- Understand the power of stories
- Know when and how to use them successfully
- Create your own stories
- Find good stories from other sources.

Storytelling is increasing in popularity in business presentations in recent years. When you think about the presentations you have seen and remembered, it is easy to work out why. I bet you remember the stories quicker than the facts. If you were to sit and watch a presentation loaded with facts and figures, even if it is well delivered, it is hard to take it all in, whatever about remembering it. If you listen to a well-crafted story that is told sympathetically, it has you riveted. This helps you to listen more carefully to what is being said. Remember, when you were a child and your parents or a teacher said, "Let me tell you a story," what happened in your brain? You probably relaxed and let the story take hold. You know this is going to be a comfortable experience – even if the story hasn't got a happy ending.

Why Stories Work

Stories tap straight into the emotions, by-passing the analytical part of the brain, and so can be powerful ways of influencing your audience. Because they can use all of the senses – visual descriptions, hearing (different tones of voice) and feelings – they appeal to all senses. This makes them memorable. Stories can be even more memorable if they are interesting or funny, as the audience repeats them afterwards. After each telling, they remember more about your presentation and they are also spreading your message for you.

Stories can also create suspense that makes us want to listen – eager to hear what happens next. If told well, they can be captivating. Stories move people to a young state of awareness, unlike other parts of a

presentation, as this is where we come across stories first. This state can be less analytical, more receptive and better connected to their unconscious and imagination. This allows you and your message to enter their minds. There is evidence to show that an engaging story will lower the blood pressure and slow your heartbeat.

Facts do not usually change an audience's mood but you can change the state of your audience with a story. For instance, the statistics of homelessness may not have much of an effect by themselves but telling a story about a real homeless person can really bring them alive. By telling an uplifting or a funny story, you can create a state of joy, a sad story can bring tears to their eyes or an optimistic story can help them to be hopeful.

> ***Word to the Wise***
>
> You can change an audience mood with a story – this is much more difficult just using facts.

It is well known that selling a product is easier if you can demonstrate it, but it is not possible to do this with many of the products or services we try to persuade our audiences to buy. But a story can demonstrate their use or misuse very well. When we try to tell a group of our staff what we want them to do, they may not agree or even refuse. A story can sometimes avoid a power struggle. When you use a story to get across a message, the audience can make up their own minds, interpreting the story the way they want to.

If you tell a story about a personal experience, particularly an embarrassing situation you were in, it can help to form a connection between you and the audience. It can help to make you vulnerable to them.

Most of us will remember stories like "Goldilocks and the three Bears", "Cinderella" and "Little Red Riding Hood". We may not remember all the facts in the right order, but we will remember the main story line. In business presentations, you can use stories to get a main theme across, or even weave facts into the story to make sure your audience remember the facts too.

Stories are more persuasive as we are asking listeners to make up their own minds rather than telling them what to do. They therefore are a more powerful influencing tool than rules and regulations. They grab your audience's attention because they are different and your audience is not expecting you to tell stories at a serious business presentation.

Types of Stories

There are three main types of stories which are useful in business presentations: stories from your own life, stories about your organisation and folk or traditional tales.

Stories from your Own Life

Some very powerful learning stories come from your own life. What happened to you? What were key learning events in your life? What were the incidents that left a lasting impression? All of these types of stories can be used to influence others to think differently and leave them with a lasting lesson they can refer back to.

Try creating a time line to find your own key stories. Take a blank sheet of paper and draw a line across the middle, starting with your earliest memory and finishing with today. Then think back to the various times in your life that were significant for you. You may include things such as your first day in school, the day you got married, the day your first child was born and other big occasions. Draw these along your time line roughly when they happened relative to other events. Then go back and add in the smaller incidents, such as the day you got lost in the supermarket, your first kiss, the day you discovered there was no Santa Claus and other smaller but equally momentous events for you.

Some people will write for hours, happily jotting down hundreds of incidents; others will find this excruciatingly difficult. If you are finding it tough, try thinking of one place at a time. For instance, thinking of the time you lived in a particular house will bring back certain memories, or when you went to a particular school, the different jobs you did or even different holidays you went on. This will help you to flesh out your list. Keep on moving through the main places in your life and then move on to different people you knew. Any stories associated with your parents, brothers, sisters, particular friends, spouse or partner. This will give you a different spin on your stories. Try all sorts of different ways of cutting it and after a while you will have a rich fund of stories to draw on.

Now go back over them and see if any of them taught you a particular lesson you learned, helped you to get over a specific obstacle, changed the way you thought about anything.

Next, choose a story you would like to work on. You need to flesh it out a little. You can do this on your own, but you will have better results if you get a partner to help you. Sit with your eyes closed and tell your partner about your story. Brief them in advance to make sure you use all the senses in your description. You need to describe what you could see, what you could hear, what you could smell and taste and what you could touch. Also, how did you feel at the time. If you are leaving any of the senses out, get your partner to ask you questions which really get you back to that place, at that time. You will be surprised at how much you remember about incidents even twenty years earlier and some things you may not have even thought about before will come into your consciousness.

All you have to do now is to work out where you can use this story, the main goal of it and the main road map through it. As soon as you start to tell it, the details will come back to you as you have actually experienced this situation yourself.

Organisational Stories

Sometimes when you are trying to describe your company to someone who does not work there, it is hard to capture what it is really about. Sure, you can tell them the history, how it was founded, the turnover, the market share, the number of employees and what you do, but this is not really going to excite the listener enough to keep their attention and they are certainly not going to learn what your organisation is really about from this list of facts. However, if you tell a story about a particular incident that happened in your company, explaining how different people reacted to events, weaving the facts through the story, it describes the culture of your organisation much better.

> **Word to the Wise**
>
> Telling a story about your organisation instead of giving factual information can give your audience a much better feel for the culture.

For example, Mike Shearwood, managing director of Zara, UK and Ireland, faced this exact problem when he was asked to speak at a conference in Ireland about his company. The first time he did this, he described the history, what brands they had, described the culture, where the company was based. It was interesting, but did not grab the attention of the audience as much as he wanted, which made it hard to present. He was afraid of losing his place and leaving a vital piece of information out so felt he needed to read the presentation from a script. This, of course, meant he could not connect with his audience the way he would have liked. He did not enjoy the experience and swore for the next time he would try a different approach. We worked together on the problem and decided that a story about the opening of the Irish store would be a good way to open the presentation, particularly as it was a fascinating story and a highly successful store opening. He sat down and told me the story, over a cup of coffee. It was funny, engaging and really described the culture, strategy and core values of the company. More than anything else, it showed the passion he felt about Zara and its introduction to the Irish market. It was obvious how much he lived the values – not just told others to.

However, when he wrote out the structure and got up to present it, it turned into a bland story again, a series of incidents, one after the other. Making a presentation out of it was taking the fun out of the story. We needed to put the soul back in. I asked him to present the story more like he had when he told me about it. The main thing he had to do was ditch the notes he had written and just take a page with about six words to

help him remember the sequence. I asked him to use visual descriptions to describe the mayhem, use the voices of the people talking to him when he was having conversations and describe how it all made him feel. It worked magically.

The best part of this story was that by describing his company through the use of a story, it captured the audience, illustrated the core points he wanted to make and described the culture perfectly, all without a single PowerPoint slide. Shortly afterwards he was asked to speak at another business conference in Ireland. He used the story method. To complete the presentation, all he had to do was go over the main points he wanted to make, giving factual information and drawing illustrations from the story, and pull it all together into a main message. He was fantastic. He hardly used notes at all, captivated his audience and gave them some useful information to take away. He was the star of the show!

This type of story can also be used when presenting to a group of your own staff. Stories about how your organisation came into being, the things that have gone wrong over the years, the heroes of the company and what they did to turn a difficult situation around. They are incredibly useful for new employees to let them know the culture of the organisation they have just joined and what is valued and frowned upon.

Folk Tales and Traditional Stories

All cultures have plenty of these, none more so than the Irish. Many have morals and lessons to be learnt and can be useful in stressing important points. Grimm's Fairy Tales, Zen Stories, Irish Folk Tales, Fairy Stories are all useful in this way. You may need to read a story a few times to get the message you want from it – and don't forget, you can change these stories to suit the situation.

When you have first read through a story that you want to use, put the book away and write down the bones of the story. Try to tell it in your own words, using just the bones you have identified. Because this is not your own story, it may be harder to remember than one you have experienced so you will need to get inside it and feel it. Try drawing a map of the story so you know where the various events happened – don't worry about trying to draw the characters, stick people will do. What is important is to identify that the story moves through different places; when you are telling it, you need to know the location of these different places in relation to where you are standing. For instance, if you are telling a story where a character comes in and puts down a briefcase and later picks it up again, these two places need to be the same. If you pick it up in a different place to where you put it down, you will jar the audience out of the story. It ceases to be believable if the details are not consistent.

Then take your map and walk through it, finding all the places in the room. Pick things up and put them down again just where the characters do in the story, actually acting it out. This will ensure the story will stick in your head and you will not forget what happens next.

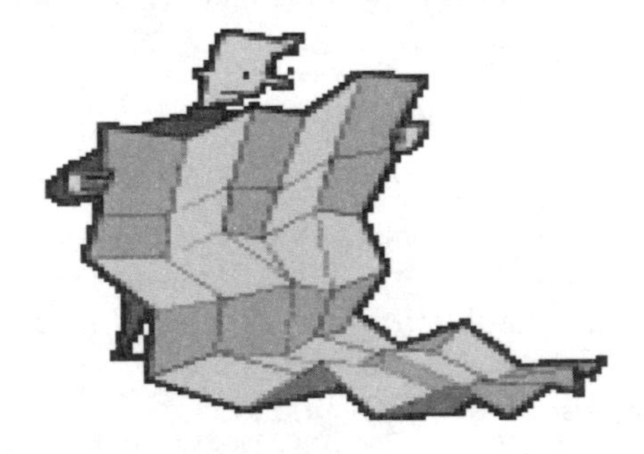

Speak the story out loud, with a friend or colleague if you can. While you are doing this, you can find the problems with the story the way you are telling it. Now you are ready to try it out on your audience.

I know all this sounds like a lot of work, but if you take short-cuts, the audience will notice as you won't be as authentic a story teller as you, or they, would like.

Pitfalls of Using Stories

Stories not told well can be limp and disappointing to your audience. You really need to work on your delivery. There are lots of areas you can work on. If your story is not relevant to your presentation, it can lead to a feeling of indifference – "so what?" If it is told well, the audience will remember the story but if it is not linked to a key point, it will not help them to remember your message. Also, if stories are too long and not well paced, people may lose the will to live by the time you have finished!

A presentation that consists simply of stories can be seen as "fluffy" or "padding" to an audience who are just interested in facts. I can remember, many years ago, running a course on customer service for a group of engineers in a manufacturing company. I used stories throughout to illustrate my points. I had found that this was a useful way to get people to understand the issues from a customer's point of view. I was disappointed at the comments I got at the end of the two days – "Too many stories". I had to re-think my approach for the next time. I realised that it was essential to balance the stories with lots of frameworks, tools and techniques to enable the engineers to get their teeth into the learning. They needed more how-to than why. The next time I worked with a similar audience, I shortened the stories and gave more frameworks and models. It worked a treat.

Stories, even more so than the presentation itself, need lots of practice and rehearsal. They do not work well if you are only telling the story in a factual way. You need to tell the story from the inside out, not from the outside in.

How to Use Stories

- You can start with a story. This can help you to open with a bang and to create dissatisfaction with the status quo, which may help you to install the need to change in your audience.

- You can top and tail your presentation with a story – start the story at the beginning, make your presentation and finish with the end of the story.
- You can tell a story during your presentation to prompt an audience discussion.
- You can tell short stories throughout to illustrate key points that you want your audience to remember.

Do's and Don'ts

Don't tell stories just to entertain the audience
Don't use stories on their own – remember, most audiences need facts too
Don't tell stories without "living" them

Do use stories often to illustrate your points
Do choose stories carefully to fit your points and your audience
Do use all communication channels to tell your story

Chapter Eight

Delivering Professionally

This chapter will help you to:

- Become aware of your body language and use it well when presenting
- Understand the need for getting good eye contact with your audience
- Use your voice powerfully to really get your message across
- Avoid annoying habits.

Making a presentation is about communicating with your audience. The better you communicate with that group of people the better your presentation will be. Dr Albert Mehrabian[1] conducted extensive studies on communication of feelings and attitudes. These were some of his findings:

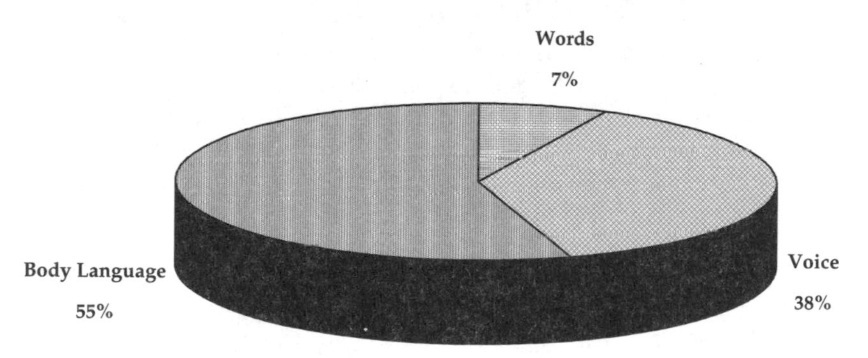

---

[1] Albert Mehrabian, *Silent Messages*, Wadsworth Publishing, 1981, pp. 76.

> ***Word to the Wise***
>
> Your body language and voice tone make up a large part of the message you communicate – use them to the full.

He believes that only 7 per cent of the emotional content of the message you send comes across in the words you use, 38 per cent depends on the tone of your voice and a staggering 55 per cent on your body language. These findings may seem a little extreme to some of you, but if you are sceptical, go and sit in an airport, bar or café for an hour and observe people communicating with other. See just how much information you can get from the body language alone. Then move a little closer and hear the voice tones; without listening to the words spoken, see how much more you can work out. The words, when you finally hear them, will not add a huge amount to your understanding.

Body Language

Notice your own body language while you are speaking. Do you stand still while you are talking to a friend or colleague or do you move your hands, arms and feet? Try describing a huge building, a tiny speck or a spiral staircase without moving your hands. Pick a common phrase like "It's a beautiful day, isn't it?" Try saying it in lots of different ways, using different body gestures, facial expressions and voice tones and see if it comes across differently to others. We all use gestures and facial expressions to get our message across while we are talking to others but for some reason most of us find it difficult to decide what to do with our hands while we are presenting. We seem to believe that we have to behave differently while we are communicating just because it is a presentation and we are on stage. The best speakers use the same gestures as they use during normal communications. The more natural you look the better. This makes you more believable and credible as a speaker. Some of us also feel we have to stand with our feet in the same place throughout our time on stage. This isn't natural either so why do it?

One of the reasons we have such a problem with our body language is that when we get nervous and the adrenalin starts pumping around our bodies, it makes our muscles slightly more rigid than usual which results in some of our movements appearing robotic. In order to avoid this effect, try shaking out your arms and legs before you come into the room to make a presentation. Excuse yourself for a few minutes and go out to the loo. Stand loosely and fling your arms out in front so that you can feel the muscles in your shoulders tense. Repeat this about five times. You should find your hands are now a little tingly. This means that if you try to use your hands to gesticulate during your presentation, your movements should be natural instead of stilted.

Try the same with your legs. Usually, the taller you are the more this is a problem for you. Your knees can lock up and you can end up walking like you are on stilts. Try standing on one leg at a time and shaking out the knee a little. This should help you to relax the muscles in your legs.

There is something about a presentation that makes us unnatural and rigid. We tend to think that we must behave in a formal manner. We even prefer to stand behind a table or lectern so that we are hidden from the audience as much as possible. This makes us feel safer but it also takes away much of our power as a presenter because our audience now cannot see our body language as easily. You are always better to come out from behind these barriers and connect more closely with your audience.

Facial expressions are also important as a means of communicating a message. When you are having a conversation with a friend or colleague, and they are doing the talking, you watch their face while listening to them. You do this because you get a lot of information from their facial expressions. Your audience does the same during your presentation. They are watching your face to get a large part of the message: if you are smiling they will get one meaning; if you are scowling, they will get another. Sometimes our faces go blank when we are nervous. This can make the audience believe that you are not interested in what you are saying and it may be harder for them to take your message on board. If you are scowling, they may find you intimidating, even though you may be scowling because you are nervous. Your facial expressions can so easily be misconstrued by your audience.

Be careful how you stand. If you slouch and lean against a wall with your hands in your pockets, it is likely that your audience will believe that you do not have much respect for them. Similarly, if you sigh and drag your feet along the ground while you are walking about, they may get the same impression.

Make sure you have your hands open towards your audience while you are talking to them, especially if you want them to join in. Some people have a fear of the question time at the end of presentations. One of the fears is that no one will ask a question. If this ever happens to you, take a look at your body language while you are saying, "Any Questions?" If you have your arms folded and your feet crossed which is quite common, you have your answer: 7 per cent of you is saying, "Any Questions?" but 55 per cent of you is saying, "Don't you dare!" No matter what voice tone you use, it is not enough to tip the balance in favour of the audience feeling comfortable about asking questions. If you really want your audience to join in, you must open your hands towards them, smile encouragingly and speak in a warm tone of voice. (See Chapter 9 for further discussion on this.)

You can make a different impression on your audience depending on the position you stand in. Family therapist Virginia Satir developed five non-verbal patterns of communication. Each of these patterns can have a different impact on your audience.

Satir's Five Non-Verbal Patterns of Communication

Leveller	Body symmetrical; hands out in front, with palms down, moving downwards and spreading.
Placater	Body symmetrical with open body language; hands in front, palms up, moving upwards.
Blamer	Body asymmetrical; leaning forward, pointing a finger at audience.
Computer	Body asymmetrical; hand on chin or arms folded – in "thinker" pose.
Distracter	Body asymmetrical; angular, disjointed and all over the place.

You can see straight away that some of these will be more useful in presentations than others.

The most useful will probably be the *Leveller*, as it gives you presence, gravitas and credibility. It is a great way to start a presentation, particularly where you are on a lower level to some of your audience or a woman in an all-male environment. Adopting this position can help you to be taken much more seriously.

Another pattern you can use to your advantage is the *Placater*, as it suggests openness and vulnerability and can be particularly useful if you need to get people on your side.

The *Computer* is a more thoughtful pose. It can help you to come across as reasonable. The image is cool, calm and collected.

Try these out and see what difference they make to the way your audience perceive you and react to you.

Eye Contact

There are two reasons why you should work on getting good eye contact with your audience. Firstly, you need to get information from them. If you look at their eyes throughout your presentation, you will know how they are feeling about the different issues you are talking about. Watch their faces as you try to explain a complicated and complex area and you will know whether they understand you. If they understand you clearly, you will see them smiling and nodding. If they are lost they are more likely to have quizzical looks on their faces. This is useful information. Make the most of it. You may notice that a large number of the group of people in front of you are drifting off – eyes glazed over, sliding down in their chairs. If this happens, stop what you are doing IMMEDIATELY. You are boring them. Recap quickly in two sentences and say you would like to move on to a different area, or suggest a quick break if that is appropriate. Whatever you do, do not continue: this would just waste your time and theirs – and they would not forgive you easily. If, however, one person is looking bored and disinterested, do not be disheartened. Maybe that individual had a late night. Be guided by the majority, however they are behaving.

> ***Word to the Wise***
>
> Making strong eye contact with each audience member flatters them and enables you to build a good relationship with them during your presentation.

The second reason to make eye contact with your audience is to show them that you are interested in them. Looking at each person in turn will make them feel included and flattered. This will help you to build a good relationship with them. Remember, people buy people. If you want them to buy what you are selling, they must buy you first. They need to like and respect you. The best way to get people to like you is to show you are interested in them. You do this mainly through eye contact. Don't just sweep past their eyes, though. You need to hold the eye contact long enough to actually connect with them. It should be like having a conversation with individual members of the audience.

Some of you may feel a little intimidated when you try to make eye contact with your audience. You will get over this. The problem is that people never see your intentions. They only see that you are not looking at them and perceive that you are not interested in them.

Be careful not to miss out on anyone. This is particularly difficult if the chairs are set out in a U-shape, for example around a board-room table. It is easy to miss out the people nearest to you. If you do not make a special effort to make eye contact with these people they may feel left out. When people feel left out they may start looking for attention in other ways. This is not always helpful to you, the presenter. This is how hostile audience members are born. To avoid creating difficult audience members, ensure you are including everyone.

You may also fall into the trap of looking at one person more often than the others because they appear to be nodding and smiling a lot or because they are the decision maker. The rest of their colleagues will resent this and again may become hostile towards you either during question time or afterwards when you have left and the decision is being made.

If you are working with a large audience, you need to keep moving around so that you can get eye contact with the entire audience, as some will be hidden behind others. The movement will also add interest to your presentation.

Using your Voice

Your voice is one of your most persuasive features. It can say so much about you and your commitment to what you are saying. I am sure you have sat through a speech where the presenter spoke in a monotone for twenty minutes and bored the entire audience to tears. The more interesting you can make your voice the easier it will be to listen to. You can use a range of tones, pitches, paces and volumes to add interest. When you are emphasising a point, you can use any of these. If you add the appropriate body language, it can be extremely powerful as a persuasive tool.

If you find you cannot easily change your voice, you can try a few solutions. A simple way of improving your voice is to get yourself a large book of fairy stories and some young children, preferably about six or seven years old. Seat them around on the floor. Sit down with them and read the stories using all the voices. Every fairy story has **great big giants and monsters** and *little teeny weeny fairies and elves.* These all have different voices.

Just think of the scope you will have with *Goldilocks and the Three Bears*! The reason you should read these to children rather than reading them on your own is this. Children absolutely love adults reading to them using all the daft voices. They smile and roll around laughing when you do this. This will give you the positive reinforcement you need to

help you increase your range of voice tones while you are presenting. Every time you use your increased range, you will remember the children's smiling faces and know it is a good thing to do.

When presenting, it is a good idea to be aware of the tone at the end of your sentences. Take a sentence such as, "So, I'd really like you to start making these changes straight away". Say this sentence and let your voice tone rise while you say the last two words "straight away" and you will notice it will sound like a question. Try it again, this time letting the tone flatten off for the last three words. This time it sounds more like a statement. Now try it once again, but with your tone falling at the end. This time, it may sound more like an order. You can play around with the voice tone in a number of ways, but always ensure it is congruent with your body language and your words so you are not giving two different messages.

Another way to help your voice is to do some voice exercises. Here are some simple ones you should do every day to keep your voice in top shape:

Jaw Drop
Let your jaw drop as far as possible, then close the mouth, repeat six times. You should feel a little sore on either side of your jaw. This will help to correct a stiff jaw.

For Flexible Lips
Repeat "ah-oo, ah-oo" several times.

Tongue Darting
To correct a lazy tongue, try shooting your tongue out as far and as hard as possible until it is tired. It will then fall naturally into its right position in your mouth. This will ensure you won't get tongue-tied.

Pitch, Pace and Pause
The best exercise for working on pitch, pace and pause is reading aloud as much as possible. Try poetry and prose, modern and old. Find pieces you like and read aloud with enthusiasm. It will have the added benefit of increasing your vocabulary and widen your knowledge of literature you can quote from during your presentations.

Breath Control
Breathe in through your nose. Breathe out with a prolonged hum, or to numbers if you like. Do not continue until you have to gasp for breath, as this can do you damage.

Try breathing in for three counts, hold breath for three counts, breathe out for three counts. Repeat, increasing the counts. Both of these exercises will help you to control your breath better when speaking.

Annoying Habits

We all have these and they usually get exaggerated when we are nervous. Have you ever noticed that other people tend to pick up a certain word or phrase and use it constantly for a number of months before they let it go and take up with a new one? You probably do this too. You need to find out what word or phrase you repeat. Typical ones are "basically", "actually", "okay", "right", "em", "lo and behold", "do you know what I mean", "like" "to illustrate my point", "for the sake of argument", "so on and so forth" and "going forward". There are lots more. If you constantly use the same word or phrase, you may find that your audience becomes distracted and spends most of the time while you are speaking, counting how many times you use your word rather than listening to what you have to say.

Other annoying habits include clicking a pen, fiddling with keys, jingling money in your pocket and scratching yourself in the same place every few seconds. My own personal habit for a while was frantically pacing up and down, not just wandering slowly around. This happened when I got extremely nervous. It got so bad that one of my colleagues told me if I didn't stop she would nail my foot to the floor. I got the message and stopped doing it. You need to find out what your annoying habit is and eliminate it from your repertoire. Becoming aware of your own words and movements while you are on your feet and being able to correct the problems while you are still there comes with time. But at the beginning you will need to rely on your trusted friends and colleagues to let you know what daft things you are up to. Alternatively, you could attend a good course on presentation skills where you will get the feedback you need.

Making Mistakes

We all make mistakes. We sometimes say the wrong thing, do the wrong thing or make a sarcastic or undiplomatic comment that we instantly regret. When you have that awful realisation that you have messed up and are waiting for the ground to open up and swallow you, don't despair. If you take one step to the side and look back at where you were just standing and say something like, "I can't believe she said that!", while shaking your head, it disassociates you with that comment and can get you out of an awkward situation. Try it – it really works!

Do's and Don'ts

Don't stand still with your hands by your sides
Don't alienate audience members by ignoring their eyes
Don't mumble or speak in a monotone

Do use the full power of your voice
Do find out what your annoying habits are and eliminate them
Do make good eye contact with everyone in your audience
Do use your body language to help express yourself

CHAPTER NINE

Working with the Audience

This chapter will help you to:

- Get involvement from your audience
- Handle difficult people successfully
- Handle questions with ease.

Involving your Audience

You may be thinking to yourself, "Why would I want my audience to get involved in my presentation?" This is a valid question. It will depend entirely on what you are trying to achieve, how you are hoping to achieve it and on your own individual style.

It is difficult for any of us to concentrate on anything for very long – most of us have an attention span of about twenty minutes. This means that if you are presenting for any longer than this you will need to add variety to your presentation. One way to add a bit of variety and to keep your audience interested is to involve them in some way.

Remember in Chapter 5 we discussed using visual, hearing and feeling to help your audience remember what you are saying? Involving your audience in your presentation appeals particularly to the feeling people among them and will add spice and interest to your entire presentation. Another advantage is that it will help take the spotlight off you for a while. This can work particularly well at the start of your presentation when you are more nervous. If you open your presentation with a question, the audience is now focused on answering your question rather than staring blankly at you waiting for inspiration. You could try asking a question such as, "How many of you have tried this product before?" This will give you a show of hands. You could go further and try asking a question that individuals in your audience will answer, such as, "How did it work for you?" You will usually get some positive responses.

There are, however, a few rules that you should stick to if you want this interaction to be successful. Firstly, never pick on individuals. If you point out one person in your audience and ask them for an opinion on what you have just said or for their feelings on a particular issue, it may be just the moment that they drifted off and are now mortally embarrassed that they have been put on the spot. They will hate you for this. Secondly, only ask unambiguous questions. It is very awkward if you ask a question that people do not understand or are not sure exactly what you are looking for.

> ***Word to the Wise***
>
> Always reward participation; this will encourage others to join in.

Thirdly, always reward participants. Whoever answers your question and whatever answer they give, do not embarrass them or belittle them in front of the whole group. Make sure that whatever answer they give is acceptable, even if it wasn't what you were expecting.

Sometimes it is better to laugh at yourself than at an audience member by saying something like, "Well I obviously didn't communicate that very well, sorry about that, let me have another go …". You can then rephrase the question so that you stand a chance of getting the right answer. Do not under any circumstances say, "No, that's not right, anyone else?" This will make the person who answered feel bad; everyone else will feel embarrassed for them and may decide that it is just too risky to join in, as the same might happen to them.

Whatever answer you get, you should smile and look interested. This will make the person who joins in feel good for doing so. You can add to this good feeling by repeating the answer out loud to make sure that everyone hears it or, even better, writing it on a flip chart or white board. Be careful here, however, to write their exact words down. If you change the words they use into words of your own it sounds as if you are correcting them. They will not like this. If they have given you a long answer you can ask how they would put that in a few words so that you can best capture it. If they are having trouble with this, you can prompt them. But always make them feel that it is their words and sentiments that are being written down. This makes them feel rewarded.

Another way to reward involvement is to refer back to certain individuals who answered your questions earlier in your presentation. For example, at the start of your presentation, you might have asked about the uses people put a particular product to and received five or six answers. If, as you cover the different uses during the presentation, you refer to Joe who has used it for this and Pat who used it for that, it is a powerful way to make these particular audience members feel involved and important. Next time you ask a question everyone will want to join in so they can get rewarded in the same way.

Handling Hostile and Difficult Audience Members

Sometimes you do not want to encourage participation. In fact, there are times when you are afraid of your life that certain people will join in. There is a variety of ways to handle these situations. Which one you choose will depend on a few factors. One of these is judging how comfortable you are with handling interaction. Some people love it; others hate it. It will depend on your individual style. It will also depend on how well you know your subject. You may find that audience participation is great on a subject you know well but if you are winging it, you become more uncomfortable. This is quite normal. Remember, you do not have to adopt the same style for every presentation. The worst thing you can do with difficult participants is to behave like a victim. You must remain in control and show that they are not giving you any trouble at all. Where possible, harness their energy and use their willingness to get involved to your advantage. Here are some behaviours that can cause difficulty.

The Know-All

You will often have a know-all in the group, someone who keeps stealing your thunder or answering every single question you ask. The first thing to think about is why they are behaving like this. Often it is because they feel they, not you, should have been asked to make this presentation and they want everyone else in the audience to recognise their superior knowledge of the topic. If this is the case, you need to flatter them. Make a point of saying something like, "Well, we obviously have an expert here, do you mind if we call on you every now and again during the afternoon to help out?" Make sure you smile warmly at them while you say this and look genuinely pleased that they are there. This usually stops them because they have now been recognised as the expert they feel they are and do not have to keep proving it. You usually won't even have to call on their "expertise", just throw a knowing glance and a smile in their direction every now and again.

The Joker

The joker can sometimes be a handful but can also be great fun if you handle them the right way. The best presentations have energy and a few laughs. The joker can provide these for you. Use their energy and sense of humour to carry the audience through. If they are genuinely funny, encourage them to join in by rewarding their jokes and one-liners. If, on the other hand, they are trying to be smart but the audience just isn't laughing, you can add a tail to their jokes which makes them funny or make some remark about their comments.

This can have the effect of the joker thinking they have said something funny and make the rest of the group laugh, so everyone wins. Whatever you do, though, do not put them down and make them feel stupid. The audience should be protected from constant, unfunny wise cracks but the joker should not be ridiculed while you are doing this. You do not have to be the funniest person in the room. Whoever makes the audience laugh is helping your presentation. Just make sure the joker does not take over. You must remain in control.

Hostility and Anger

Sometimes you may have to face a group of people who really do not like or agree with what you are saying. Again, remain in control. Do not get sucked into arguing with them. Show respect by letting them have their say. Listen to them courteously. Show understanding by reflecting back the core of what they have said. Do not get defensive. Watch the rest of the audience while your opponent is speaking and while you are speaking and judge whose side they are on. If they are clearly with you, you are in a strong position; restate what you have said and say you would be glad to talk to them about it afterwards. Then move on. If your opponent keeps coming back at you, the rest of the audience will keep them at bay. You have let them have their say, after all. Now they want to hear what you have to say.

If the audience is clearly on your opponent's side, you must be careful not to put them down in any way. Using logic, evidence and facts, talk your way through your argument. Ask them to bear with you until you have put your point across and tell them that you will be happy to answer questions when you have finished. But do ask their permission before continuing. It would be unusual for them not to grant this permission and you will then have their attention. Show genuine interest in their points by using open body language while listening and warm facial expressions. Everyone is entitled to their opinion, even if they do not happen to agree with yours.

> ***Word to the Wise***
>
> Never be afraid of audience involvement. Use their energy to add interest to your presentation.

Using Body Language to Control Difficult Audience Members

Whenever you want to get audience participation, you must use your body language carefully. Always have open hands towards your audience, uncrossed legs and a warm smile. This way, people will be encouraged to join in. The only time you change this rule is when you do not want particular group members to participate. Imagine you have an audience member who likes the sound of their own voice and jumps in first every time you ask a question. You can control this type of behaviour with your body language.

Next time you ask a question, hold out a closed palm towards this person, not in their face like a policeman but flat, horizontal to the floor. At the same time, open your other palm towards the rest of the audience, encouraging participation. This works like a dream with most people – they will not even get offended. The reason it works so well is that the person you are shutting out is not aware they are being stopped. Only their subconscious gets the message and they decide themselves that they would rather not join in this time. If, however, you do the policeman trick and put your palm flat towards their face, they will notice and will be highly offended and will more than likely try even harder to take control from you. So be careful.

Handling Audience Questions

One great fear of every presenter is that the audience will ask questions to which they do not know the answers. Never fear, help is at hand. The first thing to remember is that you do not have to know everything.

There is nothing wrong in saying, with confidence, that you do not know but that you will find out and come back to them. Another way is to open it to the rest of the group: "Have any of you come across a problem like this before?" Anyone who has will be glad to join in.

??????????

Have you ever noticed the way politicians answer questions? They very cleverly start by answering the question they have been asked but then twist the answer around to fit the question they want to answer. You can prepare for question time in advance by using this technique. Work out the questions you are likely to be asked, both those you would like to be asked and those you are dreading, and work out some good answers. Work out how to side-step some and answer others completely.

Always answer questions concisely; the audience does not want another speech while you are answering a question. This will ensure that you get to as many questions as possible. If you get asked a question you do not understand, put the blame on yourself for not understanding it and ask the questioner to rephrase it. This will save their embarrassment.

Never get defensive during question time. This is a trap that a lot of presenters fall into. You spend twenty minutes putting your argument across and an audience member questions one aspect of it. Your natural, human reaction is to defend your point of view. Resist. If you behave defensively at this time, you may lose the respect of your audience. Instead, take on board the question, listen carefully, understand their point of view and then patiently go over your point again, drawing your questioner into the conversation if you can. If you ask their opinion at this time, they will find it harder to argue with you. But always, always, behave warmly towards your questioners. They are then more likely to come around to your way of thinking very quickly. As soon as you argue with them, it will have the opposite effect and they will start to argue back.

For example, you have just made a presentation to your senior management team proposing an investment in a new piece of equipment. The financial controller asks a question about the running cost of the machine. You thought you had covered this aspect very clearly earlier on. It is tempting to answer smartly, "As I said earlier …", or get uppity with your answer and say things like, "Obviously this is going to cost a little more, but if we want to get this extra quality, we will have to be prepared to pay for it." Instead, try explaining the answer patiently and when you have finished, you can ask them questions like, "Does this seem over the top or does it appear to be reasonable value to you?" Question time is when the real character of the presenter comes out. Be measured, calm and avoid confrontations.

Do's and Don'ts

Don't be afraid of audience participation
Don't ever put any audience member down
Don't get defensive when being questioned
Don't pick on individuals

Do reward all participation
Do use the energy of the audience to lift your presentation
Do use your body language to manage audience participation
Do remain in control at all times

Chapter Ten

Using Visual Aids

This chapter will help you to:

- Choose the right visual aids for your presentations
- Use visuals to help your audience understand you
- Put together really good slides.

Visual aids should be just that – aids. All too often presenters rely on their aids too much and the slides take over. They are there to help the audience to understand what you are saying and to help them to remember your key points. Do not fall into the trap of the slides being the only thing the audience engages with during the entire presentation. If your slides are that good, why not just send them the disk and not turn up at all. The truth is that *you* are the most persuasive weapon in your armoury during a presentation, make sure you get the attention you need to do the job. Do not let your visual aids distract from your influencing ability.

So where do you start? First, work out what you are trying to say. What are your main points? What information is absolutely essential for your audience to grasp? Work out what is the best possible way to get this message across to this particular audience.

Sometimes using technology like LCD-projected slide-shows is the best method for you, other times it is most definitely not going to do what you need it to do. In fact some audiences will even be intimidated by your use of this type of technology.

The most commonly used visual aids are as follows:

- Flip-charts and white boards
- Computer slide-shows using LCD projector
- Overhead projectors
- Video.

Flip-Charts and Whiteboards

Flip-charts and whiteboards are particularly useful when you are looking for audience participation and want to capture their thoughts. Make sure you write clearly and use large writing. Use a variety of colours and always check the pens beforehand. They often run dry and then create an unprofessional image of you as a presenter. It is always best to carry your own pens around with you as part of your kit. This way you will be certain that they will work well.

The main advantage of using either of these aids is that very little can go wrong as neither depend on electricity. It is, however, difficult to make copies of your deliberations using a flip-chart unless they are typed up afterwards. If you feel this is going to be necessary, a whiteboard with a built in copier can be useful. This way you can get a paper copy of your whiteboard within minutes with the press of a button.

When you are writing on either of these tools, do not turn your back on the audience. This will break the eye contact you have built up and harm the relationship you have with them. If you are going to use a flip chart or whiteboard, practise in advance so that you can write while standing to one side.

Flip-charts can also be prepared in advance, using images and lots of colour. If you wish to build up a diagram on the flip-chart as you talk about it to your audience and are afraid you will not remember all the points, you can write the words lightly in pencil beforehand. Your audience will not see this and you will be certain not to forget an important point.

> ***Word to the Wise***
>
> Choose the equipment you use carefully – make sure both you and your audience are comfortable with it.

Computer Slide-Shows Using LCD Projection

This is probably the most common tool for using visual aids during presentations these days. It allows you to prepare good visuals in advance. However, you do need a little practise to make sure you are using it well.

These visual aids are modern, high-tech and can be very impressive. Unfortunately, they can also break down, so beware and have a contingency plan in case this happens. They are particularly powerful if you want to show step-by-step approaches and build up graphics gradually. But a word of warning: they are sometimes used just to impress and the presenter often gets sucked too far into the technology so their presence gets lost completely.

If slide-shows using LCD projection are used well, they can be brilliant, but because they are so busy, you may spend a lot of time peering into your laptop or at the screen to make sure the right things are showing. You will need a lot of practise to get them right. They are particularly good for large groups as the image on the screen is clear.

Always use a mouse or a remote mouse to change slides; otherwise you will have to stand still right beside the computer. The remote mouse needs some practise – try this out too. What I find useful is to use the keystrokes for all the functions like opening the file, starting the slide-show etc. and use the remote mouse for just going on to the next slide. If you are not that comfortable or familiar with technology, have a sheet of simple instructions beside you when you present using this visual aid. These things always seem simple sitting at your desk but when you are panicking in front of a large group of people, simple things like how to open or close the computer package you are using can be a nightmare.

Overhead Projectors

Overhead projectors are not used much now but they are a useful back-up in case of technology failure. All overhead projectors are different, so look at the one you are going to use in advance and identify where the switch is so that you are not messing about looking for it when you try to show your first slide. Overhead projectors need power to make them work; it may seem obvious but do check that it is plugged in before you start. Another likely pitfall is the bulb blowing. Most modern projectors have a spare bulb built in which can be changed at the flick of a switch. Check before your presentation that you know how to do this.

When you are using the overhead projector, stand far enough away from it so you are not blocking the screen, but not so far that you have to walk miles every time you want to change a slide. Also, stand where you can read from the screen, not from the slide on the overhead projector. Never turn your back on the audience. You should find a position where you can face your audience at all times and read the screen by just turning your head. You should read from the screen because this is what your audience can see. If you fall into the trap of reading from the overhead projector itself, it is possible that the image is not being projected onto the screen. I had a lecturer once who used to write equations on the overhead projector and expect us to follow complicated algebra, but nine times out of ten it was being projected onto the ceiling. Needless to say, his audience had very little respect for him.

Videos

Because videos can encompass the visual, hearing and feeling all at once (all your senses), they have a tendency to be remembered more easily than other visual aids. However, the audience did not come to your presentation just to see a video, so use it sparingly. The best way to use video during a presentation is to show short clips that can be used as the basis of a discussion. This will ensure that the audience watches the video and takes the key messages from it. Video clips can also be successfully brought into your PowerPoint presentation to liven it up, so you would not need separate equipment.

Making your Presentation Visual

Using your visual aids for text only is really not making the best use of the tool and is not helping your audience to get the message. Text is not a visual. Whatever type of aids you use, try to use pictures as much as possible. Remember the saying, "A picture paints a thousand words"? It's very true: using some really simple visuals can replace words, make your slides more interesting and have a lasting impression on your audience. Some examples:

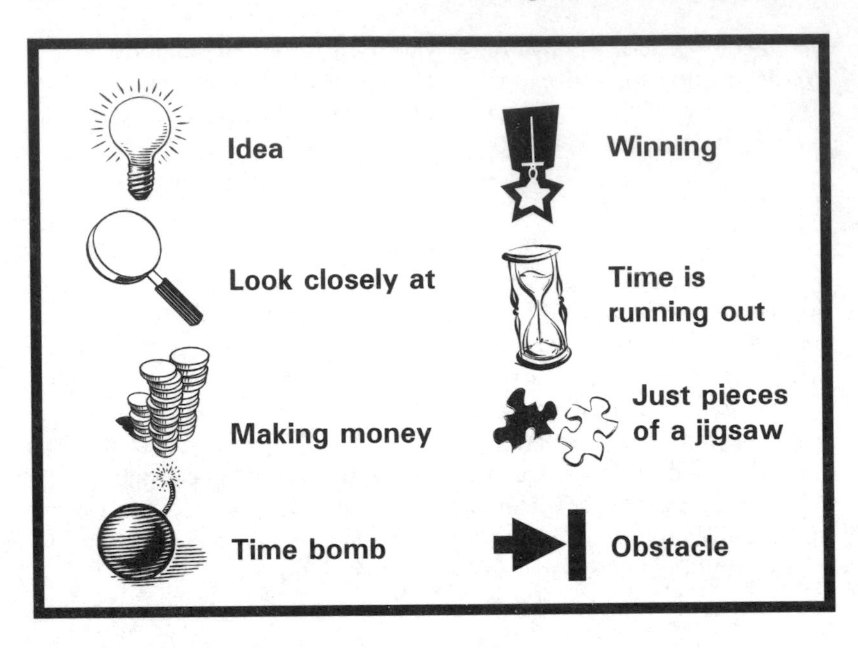

All of the above idea pictures evoke a strong message and are easily drawn by hand or by using clip art from a computer graphics package. The real trick is to be creative and make the visual do the work for you. Cartoons can work really well for some presenters but the secret to using visual aids is to use visuals that you are comfortable with. If you squirm every time you use a particular visual, it isn't for you.

Graphs

When you have figures to present, try to put them in visual format. A sea of figures is very difficult for most of us to understand; a graph showing a trend is much easier. A set of figures showing the sales of ice-cream may look like this:

	Year 1	Year 2
Jan–Feb	€3,227	€4,556
Mar–Apr	€5,632	€7,782
May–Jun	€25,088	€35,667
Jul–Aug	€27,761	€21,493
Sep–Oct	€11,913	€12,484
Nov–Dec	€13,719	€9,739

Those among us who do not work with figures as a chosen field will have to calculate the trend as we read these figures. This is hard work. However, if these were to be shown graphically, the trend is much more obvious.

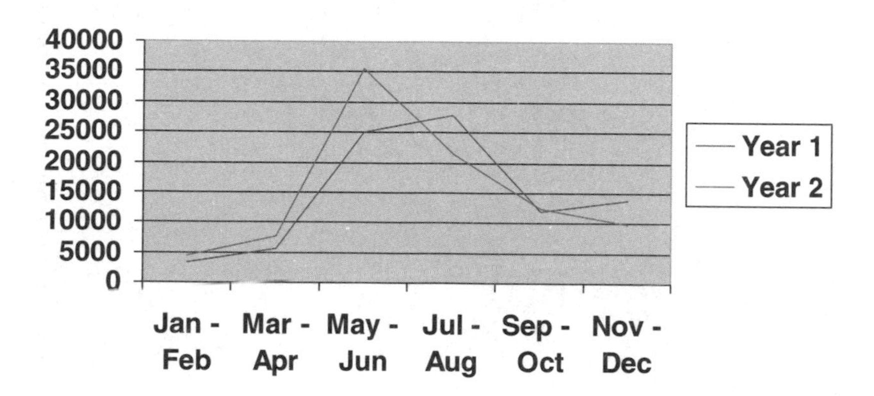

Some of the most professional visual aids are put together using a computer graphics package like PowerPoint. This can be used for either overhead slides or LCD-projected slide-shows.

> ***Word to the Wise***
>
> Keep visuals simple and visual – text is not a visual.

Making Good Slides: Ten Simple Rules

1. Keep it simple. Limit your text to bullet points. Keep editing until you have only two or three words per bullet. Never use entire sentences. These take too long to read and will take the attention away from you for too long.

2. Limit your ideas to one per slide. Do not try to achieve too much on any one slide as this will make it difficult for the audience to grasp your key point.

3. Always use a visual where you can. It will get the message across much quicker and be more memorable.

4. Create depth in your text by always using bold.
5. Use the largest font you can: 44 pt is best; 24 pt is the absolute minimum that can be read at a distance.

This is ordinary text

This is bold

6. Keep your background simple. Do not use fussy backgrounds on your slides just because they are available. Try to keep them to one plain colour. If you are using a dark background colour with light text, you will need to pick a strong, dark colour for clarity. If you want to make your background more interesting, try grading it. You can graduate the colour from dark to light in lots of different ways.
7. Choose your colours wisely. Different colours evoke different emotional responses. This is a simple chart:[1]

Colour	Emotional Associations
Blue	Peaceful, soothing, tranquil, cool, trusting
Red	Losses in business, passion, danger, action, pain
Green	Money, growth, assertive, prosperity, envy, relaxation
White	Neutral, innocence, purity, wisdom
Yellow	Warm, bright, cheerful, enthusiasm

[1] Claudyne Wilder and David Fine, *Point, Click and Wow*!!, Pfeiffer & Co., 1996, pp. 63.

Equally important is your text colour. Never use red or green as text colours, as there is a large percentage of the population who are colour blind and all that many of them will see is a blur. Use these colours as highlight colours instead.

8. Try to use serif fonts rather than sans serif. Serif fonts are those with the tails; sans serif fonts are without the tails.

d	this is serif
d	this is sans serif

We learn to read using serif fonts; we read it in books and newspapers so are used to it. It is therefore easier and quicker to read.

9. Avoid using capital letters for text, as they are hard to read. If you were to try to read a sentence written in capitals and a sentence written in lower case, you would notice that the lower case is quicker to read. This is because we learn to read this way. We recognise whole words and phrases at a time. When we read capitals, we have to read letter by letter and this is a much slower process. You need your audience to read quickly so use lower case.

THIS IS UPPER CASE AND IS SLOW TO READ

This is lower case and is much quicker

One of the reasons we use upper case on slides is because when we used typewriters, the only way to make text bigger was to use capitals. Now with word processing and graphics packages, we can make text stand out by using larger font sizes.

10. When creating slide-shows for LCD projection, you will need to add transitions between slides. These will bring you from one slide to the next. Choose the simplest ones. There are a lot of complicated, flashy transitions that will distract your audience from the slides themselves. The simplest ones fade from one slide to another.

You may also want to add sounds to your slide-show. Do not have sound on every slide – it gets annoying after a while. Use it sparingly for maximum impact, maybe on one or two selected points.

If you follow these simple rules, you will be able to make excellent slides for every type of presentation that will enhance your key points and help to make them memorable.

Do's and Don'ts

Don't use technology that you are uncomfortable with
Don't use complicated visuals to impress – they don't
Don't turn your back on the audience while you are using equipment

Do use simple visuals – complicated ones distract your audience
Do practise with your visual aids in advance
Do check out your equipment before you start

Chapter Eleven

Humour as a Tool

This chapter will help you to:

- See the advantages of using humour in your presentations
- Find the best type of humour for you and your audiences
- Find and use suitable humour.

Humour lifts people generally. Did you know that laughter is one of the best stress-busters known to man? The medical profession has been interested in this area for some time. They have even discovered that laughter not only reduces stress but also increases your resistance to infection. Just think of the good you can do by adding a little humour to those dry presentations. Laughter really is a great medicine.

> ***Word to the Wise***
>
> Laughter can help to relieve the stress in the room during a presentation.

Think about how you feel before you start making that presentation. Remember the nerves we talked about in Chapter 1? You are probably highly stressed at this point, but if you can have a laugh, your stress and panic will ease. Your nerves and those awful symptoms of nerves – shakes, wobbly voice and all the others – will abate. Now, if you stand there laughing at your own little joke, the audience will more than likely take offence or wonder what sort of lunatic you are. But if you can get them to laugh with you, you will be on the way to a stress-free presentation.

Remember, they may also be nervous. They are wondering what to expect from you. In some cases they are afraid that they won't understand what you are saying, afraid that they are wasting their time. They may also fear that you may pick on them, ask them a question they cannot answer and that they will make a fool out of themselves. Giving them a good laugh will reduce their stress levels as well, leaving them to enjoy your presentation and learn from it. It is also a well-known fact that it is easier to learn if you feel safe and are enjoying yourself.

But what if you are not a funny person – if you cannot even tell a joke to your friends successfully? Luckily, jokes are not the only way to make people laugh. In fact, I would recommend that you do not use jokes as part of a presentation. Firstly, it is far too easy to get them wrong and, if they fall flat, you end up feeling like a total fool. Secondly, they can take away from what you are saying and demean your presentation.

But don't try to tell me that you never laugh or make others laugh. We are all funny at times, sometimes when we do not mean to be. Next time you say something funny and make everyone around you roar laughing, think for a moment about what you said, how you said it and what was funny about it. Write it down; capture it for use again in a different context. When you have done this for a while, look and see if there is a trend. If there is, you now know how to make your audiences laugh. It's all about finding your own humour, what type of humour you are comfortable with and what makes people around you laugh.

There are lots of ways to lighten your presentation without losing your important message.

Cartoons

Cartoons can work extremely well as visuals. If you know anyone who is a good cartoonist, so much the better. The standard clip-art cartoons can be a little tired by now but if you can find a CDRom with cartoons that are not in constant use, these may be helpful. As with all visuals, make sure the cartoon illustrates the point you are trying to make; otherwise, although your audience is falling around laughing, they may not actually be getting the message. A word of warning: if you do not find the cartoons funny, this will come across, so don't use them unless you are comfortable with them.

Video Clips

Video clips can be a powerful way of getting audience attention and relieving the tedium of just listening to a speaker. If they are funny clips – even better. As with cartoons they must illustrate the point you are making. If you show a funny video clip it is likely to be the piece best remembered by your audience. You must ensure that they remember *why* you showed it.

Funny Stories

Funny stories are brilliant for lightening up a presentation. If you tell a story about something that actually happened to you it has an added advantage: you won't forget it and with a little rehearsal it will roll easily off your tongue. If you tell a story well, it will appeal to everyone in the audience. If you include facts and figures, visual descriptions and real feelings, you can capture all of your audience and have them waiting, with bated breath, for the punch line. Try telling your story to different people in different ways and watch the response you get. You will find some stories will be funny no matter which way you tell them, because they are just really funny things that happened. Sometimes, to add extra humour, you can exaggerate the bits you tell against yourself. This will get empathy from your audience and really get them feeling the way you did when you were in that situation. (See Chapter 7 for more on storytelling.)

Hooks

A hook is a statement or object designed specifically to get attention. We see them every day as headlines in newspapers, as trailers for television programmes or films, or as teasers for advertisements. Even the evening news programmes use them. Have you ever noticed how, just before the break, they announce what is coming up next? And there is usually a human-interest type story at the very end. This is the teaser. We have to wait right through the adverts and the second half of the news to see what it was about. Clever, isn't it?

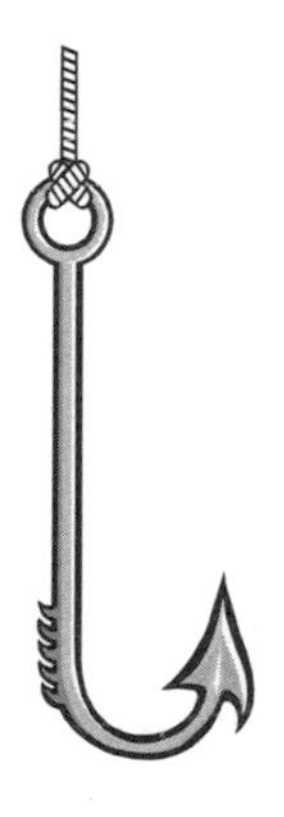

So how about hooks in presentations? Try thinking about what is the most unusual, exciting, dramatic, interesting or humorous part of your subject. See if you can reduce this to one sentence. If you can, you have a hook. But you must make sure that your hook helps to bring this particular audience towards the objective you have set.

I am sure that, like me, you often think of great ideas for hooks and stories that are really relevant when you are not trying to prepare for a presentation, only to find that when you really need one, you cannot think of a thing. To help me get over this, I keep a little red book with me for jotting down ideas that occur to me when I least expect them. This little book is invaluable as a source of ideas for these stories and hooks. One area I teach a lot is customer service. You can imagine the number of examples I come across every day of interesting service (good or bad), but when I need them most, they can be a bit illusive. So I have got into the habit of jotting them down as I come across them, so that next time I need an example it is just sitting there waiting for me.

> ***Word to the Wise***
>
> Only use humour you are comfortable with; if you do not find it funny, neither will your audience.

Creating Humour

The most difficult part of using humour is to have an idea in the first place. How can you add humour to your subject? After all, it's boring, isn't it? And even if you did think of a funny story, how could you possibly get it across? You're not a clown! It's supposed to be a serious presentation. You want the audience to take it seriously, don't you? Now, I am not suggesting for a minute that you make your presentation so funny that the audience rolls around in the aisles. That wouldn't help you at all. But I am suggesting a subtle humour that will lighten the presentation from being dull and dreary to more exciting, passionate and funny.

One of the best ways to think of the funny side of your topic is to have some sort of a brainstorming session with a group of friends, family or colleagues. People who do not know much about your subject can more easily see the funny side. Do not do this in a formal way, but when you meet a group of people, throw out the subject and see what funny remarks or stories come out. You will be surprised how easily people think of these funny ideas and stories when they are not under pressure.

It has the added advantage of giving you more courage to deliver them when there are a group of people who think it is good, funny stuff. Most of us retreat into the normal, boring, formal way of making presentations because it is safe – it may not be interesting to the audience, but at least it is safe. We have to force ourselves out of this corner. We have to find the more interesting and brave way to put our message across. There is an old saying – "You can't make an omelette without breaking eggs". This is very true of presentations. Sure, if you want to take the safe option and continue to make safe, passable presentations, go ahead and do it. But if you want to make really good presentations that people will actually listen to and take notice of, you will have to break those eggs and try out some new things. And humour is a wonderful way to ensure that your audience will listen to you. After all, they will be having fun.

Apart from brainstorming with friends, there are some other great sources. Books and magazines such as *Bits and Pieces*, published fortnightly by The Economics Press Inc., or *The Executive Speaker*, published monthly by The Executive Speaker Co., are invaluable sources of interesting facts and information that are great for presentations. There are also lots of books of humorous quotations, funny poems and cartoons – all these will give you some core ideas that you can explore and treat with your own brand of humour.

Avoid off-colour humour or anything that is aimed at any particular group of people. Stand-up comics can get away with it in a night-club or on the television but at a business presentation, it is likely to go down like a lead balloon. Do not say anything that may even remotely offend, particularly if you are trying to be funny. People do not like to have fun poked at them or to be laughed at. Usually, the best target for a laugh is you – at least you know you can take it. You should also be aware that different cultures laugh at different things. A topic or phrase that is uproariously funny to one culture may be downright offensive to another. Do your homework beforehand and make sure you know the culture you are presenting to.

Delivering Humour

You must feel confident when you are delivering the funny bits; if you look nervous and afraid that it will flop – it will. Be animated, pull the necessary faces, use all the voices; this will make the story so riveting that the audience will get sucked in and hear the moral at the end. Never apologise in advance for telling a story just in case it does not come across as funny. A good funny story will work well even if the audience does not laugh. If you do get to the end of a story and there is only a polite titter from one or two people, you can make it funny for everyone with remarks like, "Well, you obviously had to be there", or, looking straight at the audience, say quietly, "You know, you really have great self control" or "My mother *really* liked that one". You may not feel comfortable using one of these lines, but if you do, they can be funny and can save you from a lot of embarrassment. But, as with all humour, only use it if it you are comfortable with it.

Always rehearse your funny stories, hooks or whatever you are going to use in advance. The best presenters will look as though the story has just occurred to them. This is not usually the case. Good presenters rehearse their entire presentation, but pay particular attention to the stories that sound like they are being told "off the cuff". This is because a story or joke if it is told badly can be a disaster. If you forget to tell an important bit at the start and get to the end and nobody knows what you are talking about, you are sunk. Then you would have to say something like, "Well, I should have told you at the start ..." Of course, if you are good at delivering stories, this would not be a problem; it would actually add to the humour of the situation, because you would be laughing at yourself. But if you get embarrassed when you make a mistake, the audience will get embarrassed too and your humour just will not work.

Do's and Don'ts

Don't use humour unless you are comfortable with it
Don't apologise for your humour in advance
Don't use off-colour humour

Do remember that laughter can reduce stress
Do have a few "saver" lines ready in case your humour does not work
Do be brave - don't always play too safe
Do get others to help you to be creative

CHAPTER TWELVE

Avoiding Pitfalls

This chapter will help you to:

- Pull it all together
- Manage your environment
- Handle problems when they do arise.

Pulling it All Together

Just as in a good presentation, a book on presentation skills needs to summarise the key points at the end. So here is a twelve-point plan for making brilliant presentations.

1. **Set a clear objective**. Know what you want to achieve and what you want to have in your audience's head when they leave the room. Be aware of what action you want them to take as a result of your presentation. Write it down on a sheet of paper and refer to it often while you are preparing.
2. **Know your audience**. Find out all you can about them. Know what interests them, what they like, what turns them on. Find out what they know already about your topic so that you can tailor your presentation to the exact group of people who will be there.
3. **Prepare your content selectively**. Only include content that will bring this particular audience towards the objective you have set. Leave everything else out. It is not relevant – no matter how interesting you find it. If it does not fit the brief, be brave and leave it out.

> ***Word to the Wise***
>
> The secret to making really good presentations is to prepare well. Always give yourself enough time to do this properly.

4. **Choose your equipment carefully**. Make sure the type of visual aids you are using enhance your message, not take away from it. Ensure it is suitable for your audience and that it will not intimidate them. You don't want to come across as too smart. However, if you are working in an industry that is highly technical, using high-tech equipment will be expected of you. Be sure you are comfortable using the equipment you choose to present with.

5. **Find a way to capture ideas and information as you think of them**. Try writing down your ideas as they occur to you and keeping them in an envelope on the corner of your desk so it is all together when you need it. Work out where your creative places are. Most of us find it difficult to have unusual or creative ideas sitting at our desks. It is more usual to have our best ideas when we are relaxed and not trying to think.

6. **Arrange your material carefully**. Pay special attention to the start and finish of your presentation. If you start in an interesting way, your audience will want to hear more. It will also help to calm your nerves for the rest of your presentation. The last few minutes of your presentation will be remembered most by your audience so make sure you summarise well and include your objective in your ending so your audience will be in no doubt as to what they need to do as a result of the presentation. Find ways to help your audience to understand and remember your key points by using acronyms, hooks, stories, analogies, examples and all three communication channels.

7. **Put together your visual aids**. Avoid using much text. Pictures are more powerful. Any text you use should be large enough for the audience to read easily and in lower case. Always get someone else to read through your slides in advance. They will probably be able to spot your mistakes more easily than you. Do this in plenty of time in case you want to make changes and corrections.

8. **Rehearse, rehearse, rehearse**. The best presentations are well rehearsed. Always run through your presentation at least once using all your visual aids and props. Try to rehearse in the place you are going to present or at least in a similar venue. Do not run through your final rehearsal sitting at your desk: things are much different when you are standing up with your equipment beside you. Work out contingencies for anything that could go wrong in advance of the presentation. This way you will not be thrown as much if they happen.

9. **Develop stories** from your own life by drawing a life line. Think of useful stories from your organisation that will explain the culture and define what you do and why you do it. Read through books of folk and traditional tales to find suitable learning stories which you can use in your presentations.

10. **Be aware of the first 30 seconds** of your presentation. Manage your emotional state in advance: only say positive things to yourself and wipe out all negative self-talk. Learn to breathe well and take a few deep breaths before you stand up to speak. Just before you stand, take a last deep breath and breathe out as you stand up, making sure your eyes are looking straight ahead and connecting with your audience. Make sure your centre of gravity is low in your body – about three inches below your belly button – and walk confidently up to start.

11. **Deliver professionally**. Be aware that nerves are important for making a good presentation but be able to manage the downside of the jitters. Knowing that you can manage and hide your nerves from your audience will help to settle you down. Be ready with a good, strong opening and deliver it with confidence. Work out in advance where you are going to stand, where you will put your notes and slides and how to work the equipment.

    Do not have pens, paper or anything else in your hand while you are presenting, as it will prevent you from using your body language successfully. Maintain good eye contact with all of your audience throughout and keep your voice interesting by using the full range of tones and volumes. Use body language and rewards to manage audience interaction and answer questions honestly and concisely.

12. **Review each presentation afterwards**. Note what went well and what you should change for next time. Ask a trusted colleague for feedback if you can and keep learning. Every time you make a presentation, you can make a better one. Remember, presenting is a learned skill.

Managing your Environment

A good presentation can be ruined by an inappropriate or unmanaged environment. Your presentation may be very interesting but your audience may still go asleep because the room is stuffy or too warm and the chairs uncomfortable. A little time spent ahead of the event can pay enormous dividends. Unfortunately, you cannot always manage the environment –

for example when you are presenting on the premises of a client or potential client – but at least thinking about some of these elements in advance can help. Here's a checklist of useful things to look at beforehand.

Word to the Wise

Don't leave anything to chance – try to think of all the things you may have a problem with in advance and solve the problems before they happen.

Room Layout

When you look at an empty room it can often seem enormous, but when you start filling it with chairs and tables you will be amazed at just how small it becomes. You will obviously need a larger room if you intend having desks for your audience. Remember, you will need a good amount of space at the top of the room so that you can move about without being on top of your audience.

The best room layout for presenting is one where you can see all of your audience at the same time. A U-shape is preferable for a small or medium number whereas some sort of auditorium with tiered seating can be useful for a large group. If you are using a room with an open U-shape set-up, make sure you have plenty of empty space for yourself in the middle. Do not get trapped behind a table. Find a small table for your laptop so that you are not stuck behind another barrier.

The most difficult layout to work with (but unfortunately the most often used) is a room with an unmovable large board-room table in the middle of it with your audience seated around it. This puts a barrier straight away between you and them and makes your job more difficult. But if that is where the presentation has to be held, then you have to live with it. Try to make a space for yourself where you can move around and maybe use a side table for your notes. Encourage your audience to move away a little from the table so that they will be more comfortable.

Avoid podiums and lecterns where possible. Again, they act as a barrier. In other words, the less there is between you and your audience, the better. If you are using a hotel or conference centre for your presentation, send them a layout plan in advance and indicate which end of the room you want everything to be. You would be surprised at the different interpretations of your telephone instructions. Half-an-hour before you start to present is not the time to discover that they got the wrong end of the stick and all the furniture and equipment has to be moved.

Ventilation and Lighting

A warm, stuffy room is a nightmare for you and your audience. Always check where the controls are for the air-conditioning, heating system or windows before you start. Try out your visual aids before anyone else arrives. This is the time to discover that your slides do not show up because the light at the front of the room is too bright. Find out how to change this. Sometimes, in hotels, the light switches are in a different room or in a cupboard, which can cause embarrassment in front of an audience if you cannot find them.

Noise

Always ensure when you are arranging to use a room for a presentation that you will not be disturbed by noises from a nearby kitchen, bar, function room or lift, particularly when you are working in a hotel. Similarly, you need to check that they will not be cutting the grass, cleaning the windows or using a pneumatic drill right beside where you will be working. I worked in a conference room in the front of a hotel some years ago when, all of a sudden in the middle of the afternoon, we got a fifteen-minute rendition of some tune being played extremely loudly on the bagpipes right outside our window. The piper was there to pipe all the guests in for a wedding. Not wanting to spoil the happy couple's big day, we took our tea break a little early but now I check this sort of thing out beforehand.

Power Sockets

If you are bringing any equipment with you, it is always safer to have a four-way plug board with a long lead as part of your kit. This way you will not have a problem with moving equipment around or setting up two or three pieces of equipment at the same time.

Interruptions

Check that any phones in the room you are using are switched off and that there is a "do not disturb" sign on the door. You should talk to reception, the porters or conference organisers to make sure that the presentation will not be disturbed once it starts. Make sure you know when and where tea, coffee and lunch breaks are to be held, otherwise you may get a knock on the door at a critical moment and a porter arriving with a tray of rattling cups and steaming pots of tea and coffee. There is nothing more distracting to an audience than the waft of hot scones straight out of the oven and French coffee. You may find they lose interest in what you have to say very quickly.

Flip-Chart Pens

Always, always bring your own. Never trust anyone to provide you with what you are expecting. You would be amazed at what some conference centres will give out for poor, unsuspecting presenters to write with. Flip-chart pens should be part of your standard kit. You can use a flip-chart if your other equipment breaks down by writing key words and drawing simple diagrams.

Technicians

Have the name and number of a good audio-visual technician with you just in case of breakdowns. The fact that you have a back-up will help your confidence in the equipment, even if you never have to use it.

Coping when Things Go Wrong

When you are making presentations, things will go wrong. Have you ever gone through a day at work, doing your usual job, when nothing at all has come unstuck, when nothing has gone wrong and you have not made a mistake? If you have, you are a very lucky person. Most of us come up against problems constantly but they don't throw us. But when these same problems happen when we are presenting they can cause us to panic. The main thing to remember is you are not infallible – nobody is. Your audience does not expect you to be perfect. In fact, if you were perfect, your audience would probably not like you. This makes you a little inhuman.

Expect things to go wrong, plan contingencies for when they do, do not get rattled and you will find presenting much easier. It is what you do to get out of your dilemmas while you are presenting that is of much more importance and interest to your audience than the fact that you made the mistake in the first place.

Learn to laugh at yourself and your mistakes. Get the audience to join in. Never blame anyone else. I hate to see presenters standing in front of an audience blaming their secretaries for spelling mistakes, technicians for equipment breakdowns or conference organisers for not giving them enough time to explain their topic well enough. These are *your* responsibilities. An audience will not like you if you try to blame others. Just make sure you check everything in advance.

Have a back-up of your notes and slides, know who to ask when you are in trouble, know where the toilets are and relax. Enjoy yourself – presenting is fun. You get a great buzz when it goes well and if you follow the tips in this book and get plenty of practise, there is a very good chance that it will. Good luck and, to use an acting expression, break a leg!

Do's and Don'ts

Don't ever blame anyone else for problems
Don't expect to be perfect
Don't leave anything to chance

Do have contingency plans for as many potential disasters as possible
Do check out your venue in advance and know how to work all the controls
Do relax and enjoy yourself – presenting can be fun

Further References and Resources

Books and Newsletters

Brandt, Richard C., *Flip Charts – How to Draw Them and How to Use Them*, Pfeiffer, 1986

Colgross, Michael, *My Lesson with Kumi: How I Learned to Perform with Confidence in Life and Work*, Grinder, Delozier & Ass., 2000

Parent, Joseph, *Zen Goff: Mastering the Mental Game*, Random House, 2002

Parkin, Margaret, *Tales for Trainers: Using Stories and Metaphors to Facilitate Learning*, Kogan Page, 1998

Townsend, John, *The Business Presenter's Pocketbook*, Management Pocketbooks, 1985

Walters, Lilly, *Secrets of Successful Speakers: How you Can Motivate, Captivate and Persuade*, McGraw-Hill, 1993

Westcott, Jean and Jennifer Hammond Landau, *A Picture's Worth 1,000 Words: A Workbook for Visual Communications*, Pfeiffer, 1997

Wilder, Claudyne and David Fine, *Point, Click and Wow – A Quick Guide to Brilliant Laptop Presentations*, Pfeiffer, 1996

Bits and Pieces, published fortnightly by The Economics Press Inc., Fax: +44 (0) 1727 844388; e-mail: 100660.2061@compuserve.com

The Executive Speaker, published monthly by The Executive Speaker Co., Fax: Ohio 937-294-6044; e-mail: mail@executive-speaker.com; Website: www.executive-speaker.com

Courses

Presentation Skills courses run by Lynda Byron at the Irish Management Institute, Sandyford Road, Dublin 16.
Telephone: (01) 207 8447
Fax: (01) 295 5150
E-mail: lynda.byron@imi.ie

Presentation Skills: an intensive two-day course, run regularly from September to June. The emphasis is on building confidence and preparation.

Advanced Presentation Skills: an intensive two-day course, run bi-monthly. The emphasis is on impact and delivery.

Index